IMPERFECT

SANJAY MANJREKAR IS a former Indian cricketer. He played for India for nine years, scored all his Test centuries abroad, and was known as a very technically correct batsman. He chose to retire at the age of thirty-two. He represented India in two World Cups – 1992 and 1996 – and was a Ranji Trophy–winning captain for Mumbai. Today, he is a popular cricket pundit known for his sharp observations and cutting-edge analysis.

Praise for *Imperfect*

'Make no mistake, this is no airbrushed hagiography dressed up as a biography. Sanjay Manjrekar's account of his career humanises the cutthroat world of international cricket. The beauty of *Imperfect* is that unlike Manjrekar's batting, it often plays outside the V. It indulges in lofted strokes and doesn't run on unexpected lines. This is where the autobiography may appeal to connoisseurs as well as commoners' – *Hindustan Times*

'A remarkable book, not for any literary flourish, but for the sheer honesty that serves as its spine. [*Imperfect*] is an endeavour that doesn't airbrush the subject ... There is so much that clogs a player's mind and in laying that back-story bare, Manjrekar has humanised the cricketer' – *The Hindu*

'A treat for the tragics ... The triumph of *Imperfect* is in the way it humanises the world of professional cricket. The battles may be of a different order, but they are battles nonetheless' – *Mint*

'Is *Imperfect* the most honest book to come out from an Indian cricketer over the last four-five years? Possibly. But this much is certain: in truth and in tenor it is most certainly the kind of book you wish every Indian cricketer would write' – ESPNcricinfo

'Among the most significant books on Indian cricket, not least for its candour, a feature sadly missing in most autobiographies, of cricketers and politicians alike ... *Imperfect*'s seminal contribution, though, is the spotlight Manjrekar trains on the human mind, the horror it can become' – Firstpost

'Lucid and precise, the book does not waste words. It holds your attention right through the 200-odd pages' – *The Week*

'An incredibly candid confession of the highs and lows in his life, of living with Vijay Manjrekar his father and a legendary Indian cricketer but also a violent and abusive man, of going through the ropes of Indian cricket, of seeing, as a Mumbai batsman, the advent of Sachin Tendulkar and now of his life as one of India's leading cricket commentators' – NDTV

'*Imperfect* surpasses all expectations. Written with honesty that is rare among celebrity authors, Manjrekar analyses himself as a person and his cricket career with an unsparing eye' – *The Sunday Standard*

'A perfectly crafted candid memoir' – *The Hindu Business Line*

'For young cricketers there is much to learn from *Imperfect*. The importance of fitness, the need for level-headedness and good, strong guidance in the early years of development, the dangers of pride and ego, the pitfalls that accompany all glamorous international sporting careers, the dangers of well-intentioned but completely inaccurate advice...' – *Asian Age*

'*Imperfect* is a must-read for players as well as fans of the gentleman's game. It is brutally honest, candid, transparent and racy' – Sportskeeda

SANJAY MANJREKAR

IMPERFECT

Harper
Sport

First published in hardback in India in 2017 by Harper Sport
An imprint of HarperCollins *Publishers*

HarperCollins Publishers India, Cyber City, Building 10-A, Gurugram, Haryana-122002, India
www.harpercollins.co.in

2 4 6 8 10 9 7 5 3 1

This edition published in paperback in India in 2019 by Harper Sport
An imprint of HarperCollins *Publishers*

P-ISBN: 978-93-5302-614-1
E-ISBN: 978-93-5277-452-4

Typeset in 11.5/16.3 Minion Pro at
Manipal Digital Systems, Manipal

Printed and bound at
MicroPrints India, New Delhi

MIX
Paper
FSC FSC® C218906

This product is made of FSC®-certified and other controlled material.

HarperCollins Publishers, Macken House, 39/40 Mayor Street Upper, Dublin 1, D01 C9W8, Ireland

To my mother

CONTENTS

AUTHOR'S NOTE

THE MOST THRILLING moment in my life is when a good movie is about to start, and I am in front of a screen in a dark room with a drink and popcorn in hand. That's my bliss.

If my father had not been a former Test cricketer, and if I had not grown up in Dadar, where the only sport people played was cricket, I would not have become a cricketer.

Since the day I retired from cricket I have not been tempted, even once, to pick up a cricket bat and play a match. I realize now, seventeen years after quitting the game, that I played cricket because it served a purpose at the time and not really because I deeply loved the game. No amount of coaxing has got me to play a cricket match after my retirement, whether it is a benefit match or a veteran's tournament or an overseas tour of retired or tired cricketers.

When I quit cricket I desperately started seeking out people who were not cricketers. They might have been related to cricket in some way, but they were not cricketers per se. I was easily impressed by seemingly knowledgeable people and surrounded myself with them, because I knew they would tell me things I didn't already know. By then I was starved for the knowledge of the world outside cricket because I had missed out on all this information. By the age of thirty-two, I was in some great hurry to catch up and get to know everything there was to know in the non-cricketing world.

Music and movies took up a lot of my post-retirement time. I have watched almost all BBC films on life, wildlife, nature, the solar system and the universe. When I watch movies, I look for ones that will educate me, show me things I haven't known or experienced, make me feel new emotions. In this pursuit, I didn't realize when I slipped into the world of foreign language films. Foreign cinema is a whole new world that I get terribly excited about – after all, it's a trip into the unknown.

I have not read a single book on sport or a sportsman's autobiography. Such books hold no interest for me, perhaps because I feel they may not reveal anything new. For example, I have no idea what's happening in the world of tennis, or in the English Premier League. When people around me talk about football and tennis, despite being a former international sportsman, I just sit silently in one corner of the room. But ask me anything about Kishore Kumar, Lata Mangeshkar, Mehdi Hassan or Nusrat Fateh Ali Khan, and we may be talking for hours.

Similarly, I consider film-makers nothing short of magicians or wizards. I have learnt a lot about life from movies. I mostly watch serious, true to life, drama; and many of them have taught me some important life lessons. A good movie for just Rs 500 is the greatest deal you can get in today's world. I never discourage my kids from watching a good film. They too have become movie buffs like me. My daughter Devika and I have passionate discussions on films we have both watched.

I must have watched most of the good Hollywood and European films. A lot of people around me share this passion. If you are a fan of films from anywhere around the world, you can be my friend. If you are a fan of Kishore Kumar, well, you can be my soulmate.

But let there be no misunderstanding. Cricket still holds a great interest for me, even if it's only in a way any job does for a working professional. The game is important for my livelihood because of the profession I have chosen after my retirement. I will forever be grateful to the sport for helping me raise my family well and give my kids a good education. If it didn't help me in my 'work', I would easily skip watching an ongoing match and instead watch a Quentin Tarantino film again. If I'd been born in a family of musicians or film-makers I'd have grown up to be one of them – maybe a good one at that – because music and cinema are the loves that have stayed and will stay with me forever.

To those who think that I underachieved as a cricketer, I say this: For a guy who was basically not really that into sport, playing more than 100 international matches was not such a bad effort, was it? You perhaps think an unfulfilled career has made me grow cold towards cricket, maybe even resent it. I have asked myself this question, and I've found the answer in the privacy of my farmhouse with only my family for company. When my son wants me to join him for a game of cricket or football, I look at him as if he has asked me to climb a mountain. I feel like saying, 'If you want my company, son, how about watching a film together?'

I think I am a bit of a geek born into a cricketing family, in a cricket-loving place, who found cricket to be a convenient career path. I can leave emotion aside when I analyse cricket. Cricketing technique and statistics fascinate me. I enjoy spending time with statisticians on all productions of live cricket.

As a kid, I played cricket because it was fun, but more so because I saw my father as a cricketer and witnessed his fame. I saw how people would turn up and take his autographs. I also watched other cricketing stars – Sunil Gavaskar, Gundappa Viswanath, Erapalli Prasanna and Rohan Kanhai – turn up on occasion at our house in Dadar. I saw people mob them outside our house.

As a child I wanted to be like them. I wanted to be famous.

This book is about me, my cricket career, my life. My strengths and weaknesses, my successes and failures. It's about my experiences. I feel we have an obligation to the next generation to chronicle our lives. Every individual lives a uniquely different life. He does not need to be famous to share his life experiences. Life stories are always interesting. No one leads an uneventful life.

Having been a sportsman, I also want young aspiring sportsmen to learn from my career. Like a father said to his son: 'I made twenty mistakes in my life; you'll make twenty new ones.'

1
MY FATHER

I HAD NO relationship with my father to speak of. The overpowering emotion that I felt towards him was fear. It is easy for me to say it now as a fifty-year-old father of two, but as a child, an adolescent and a young adult, I was terrified of my father. I have made peace with it for a long time now. Vijay Laxman Manjrekar, who played 53 Tests for India and notched 3,208 runs at an average of 39.12, was a troubled soul post retirement. A disturbed, frustrated and angry man is what his three children had as a father.

Yet, he would often be a profoundly wise man. In the few conversations that we had, he would tell me, 'Treat cricket as a game, not as your life.' He obviously said this from his own life experiences. We, his family, could see that he had made cricket his life. He was not quite prepared for life outside cricket. It's sad that in this sport you can, at best, have a career at the top for ten to fifteen years, and even that career comes to an end in the prime of your normal life, in your mid-thirties. My father had no other skills; he struggled to find his place in the world after his playing days, and that included the cricketing world too.

He was a highly respected and famous cricketer. Life after cricket must have been tough for him. He now had to work nine-to-five in a public-sector company, but at heart he was an artist. It was like asking a lead guitarist to sit behind a desk and do a clerk's job. He tried, but he wasn't cut out for it.

At one stage, he tried his hand at cricket coaching, but he didn't possess the tact required to handle young cricketers. A story goes that once former India opener Chetan Chauhan came to him for some advice. 'Sir, what's wrong with my batting?' Chauhan asked. My father told him, 'There is nothing wrong with you, but something is wrong with the selectors: they picked you.'

The coaching stint came to an abrupt halt: On a tour to England as coach and manager of the India Under-19 team he slapped a player. He never got the job again. The player in question was well known to my dad, and he didn't mind it at all, but the media was not going to let this pass. Moreover, it infuriated him that he was not famous any more and had no skills outside cricket to earn him the respect he once commanded as a cricketer.

Of course, all this I came to realize only much later. As a child, I– along with my mother and two sisters – only remember having to bear the brunt of his mood swings and temper. We lived in the fear of showdowns – often it made us dash towards the windows to close them lest the neighbours heard us. Some of these showdowns even got violent.

There was road rage too. My father would frequently get into fights with other motorists. And when I say fights, I mean it literally – ones that involved an exchange of blows. He prided himself in having earned his driving licence in England, and could not tolerate undisciplined drivers on Indian roads. Another thing that would really rile him while driving was the high beam of headlights from the car(s) behind his – its reflection in the rear-view mirror would go straight into his eyes. Whenever this happened, we would all tense up. We knew where this was all going to lead. He would then start waving his hand vigorously out of the window, asking the driver behind him to lower his beam. We would start praying, 'Please do it, please do it.' As with most prayers, this would never work. At some point, my father would allow that driver to overtake him. Then he would speed up to be within shouting distance. Then, in the choicest Marathi, my father would tell him what he thought of him. Some of the motorists would speed away out of fear, but there were always enough people to give it back to him. And then all hell would break loose.

My father would stop the car, step out, and from the boot of the car take out something called as a crook lock. It was a device he had bought from England. It was made of solid, heavy iron. It was about four feet long with umbrella-like hooked handles on both sides. One end of it was meant to be stuck in the steering wheel, and the other around one of the pedals of the car – the clutch, the brake or the accelerator. It was a security gadget against car theft, but it hardly protected my father's car. Instead it lay silently in the boot of the car until it was called upon to inflict injury on another human being.

Fortunately, my father never managed to land a serious blow with that Crook Lock as invariably a crowd would gather around such a scene. That ensured the fight ended with only some grappling and some missed punches. My sisters or my mother would sometimes get out of the car to calm him down and pull him back inside the car, but an angry man is a strong man and these attempts were largely unsuccessful.

My father was oblivious to the devastating effect such scenes had on his family. The result – we lived in constant fear and tension when he was among us. As a kid, whenever I heard his car enter our residential premises, and then heard the car door slam and the doorbell ring, I'd jump into bed and pretend to be asleep. I'd wake up only when he'd left.

But to be fair, my father wasn't alone in his frustration with Mumbai's traffic. Like him and most Mumbaikars, I too sometimes let the city's traffic get to me. It is hard not to. Once, even I lost my temper. Fuming, I didn't even realize when I'd got out of my car and grabbed the collar of the offending driver, a cabbie. For some reason, exactly at that moment, I cast a glance towards my car and saw the shocked faces of my wife and my then six-year-old daughter. In that very instant I saw my adolescent self and my mother in my father's car. It jolted me out of my state of fury and I let go of that man.

This was fourteen years ago. Ever since I have never let my irritation on the road get the better of me – it remains the only time I ever got into a physical altercation with another person.

My father could also be an emotional man sometimes, one who wasn't shy of expressing his love for his family. He would often bring us gifts and treat us to Chinese meals at Flora restaurant. Despite all his flaws, he was loyal and committed to my mother. He would stick it out with his family no matter how challenging the circumstances. He was also an extremely generous man. He'd keep loose change tied up in a handkerchief inside his drawer, perhaps for emergencies. I remember when he was hospitalized for a long time, I stole from there; it was for a hotdog they served in the school canteen, that I couldn't have afforded otherwise. When he was discharged, he came home and saw his stash of coins had disappeared; he asked me if I had taken it. I said yes. He asked me why. I told him. He didn't say a word.

However, it was his short temper that overshadowed such tender moments. All his three children – my sisters, Shubha and Anjali, and I – have grown up to be reasonably healthy adults physically. We are now parents ourselves, but each of us still carries the scars of that childhood. It is evident through different traits, traits that may not be obvious to the outside world; but we can easily see them in each other while we go about our daily lives as adults. Perhaps it showed in my batting – observers of my game thought I was overcautious as a batsman, that I could have played with a little more freedom. Maybe they were right. Maybe my game reflected the way I grew up as a child.

I have often been told that carrying the weight of my father's name bogged me down as a cricketer. They said that upholding the legacy of the Manjrekar name was never going to be easy and I was always bound to suffer by comparison. I, however, hardly knew my father as a cricketer and was never conscious of my last name. So overwhelming was his personality that I don't quite remember how he was as a cricketer. My strongest memory of him as a cricketer is of a person who cared a lot about the game. But he was retired by then. He played typical post-retirement cricket at Shivaji park. He was unfit and overweight, but I remember him in white immaculate clothing, always. It took me a long time to realize he was an exceptional cricketer. When he used to bat, I didn't care to watch him. I just knew that I had a cricket dad, and when I'm quizzed more about him today, all I can volunteer is that he used to be a cricketer.

Only when I became old enough to analyse people's awe – I'd often be introduced as Vijay Manjrekar's son – did I realize that he must have been special, that I might be something special by association. When you look at his cricketing record, you wouldn't put him among the greatest Indian batsmen, but his former teammates and fellow cricketers always held him in the highest regard. Every time I meet Erapalli Prasanna, he tells me he worshipped my father's batting. I know he doesn't say these things just because I am Vijay Manjrekar's son. He has said it on all platforms: Vijay Manjrekar was the best batsman that he bowled to. Mansur Ali Khan Pataudi, who neither has agendas nor beats around the bush, said that he was the best Indian batsman he'd seen.

My father's contemporaries would tell me that he had a great sense of humour and ready wit. The 'Vijay Manjrekar stories' are legendary in Mumbai cricket circles. (Once an opposition batsman asked him if he could change his bat, and he said, 'Please do that, and while at it, change your batting too.')

The funniest ones, though, are best not reproduced in print. As his son, I feel quite proud narrating these stories to new listeners. Every time I tell them, I get a better understanding of how he thought as an individual, and how different I am in comparison. He was the typical Shivaji Park–bred, brash, naughty guy, one who escaped from the boarding school in the coastal village town of Bordi, Maharashtra, where his parents had sent him because he was unmanageable at home. I took more after my mother, Rekha, who was soft-spoken, did things in an orderly manner, and stared blankly when my father cracked one of his jokes. His attitude to the game was perhaps better than mine. He had a certain amount of cockiness on the field against the opposition, and he was a bit more street-smart than I was. I was perhaps more sensitive than him. Perhaps that was my biggest weakness – I was very sensitive to external factors.

Quite remarkably, my father never interfered with my cricket. In fact, he was quite unaware of my cricket. The poor man was too caught up with his own problems to be bothered about me. Rarely would he ask me which match I was going for, when he would see me step out of the house in my whites. That rare match would then become the biggest match of my life. At some level I am grateful he didn't get too involved in my cricket; if he had, I would have perhaps never made it as a cricketer.

I remember the day when he suddenly said to me, 'I am coming with you to your nets, and may bat a bit myself.' I was completely taken aback. I just could not imagine him with me in the same nets along with my friends. I cringed at the thought, knowing it was going to be the single-most awkward experience of my life. I also could not imagine just him and me in the same car for all that time while we drove to the ground. So, I did what children do – I fled from the scene.

Around practice time I went missing so that he would not find me. I hid on the terrace of our house for hours, and finally appeared in front of him only when it was night. Surprisingly he did not make a big issue of it. He just asked me where I had disappeared, and that he had been looking for me in the afternoon to go to the nets with me. I kept quiet. That day was the only occasion where I missed a practice session for a not-good-enough reason.

When I look back at this incident now, I know I overreacted. I feel stupid. Even on that day, I'd felt sorry for him after a while. All he had wanted to do was to go to the nets and play cricket with his son, and I did not let him have that small wish. But I was sixteen then, and that's how I felt about my father at that time.

I owe him gratitude for one thing. He instilled in me the belief that I was eventually going to become a Test cricketer. If not for that vote of confidence early in my life, I would not have been single-minded in my pursuit of playing for India. When I was in college, in class XI, a fellow student asked me what I was planning to be in life. I said 'cricketer', and he said, 'What if you don't become one?' I had no answer to that. I had not given that possibility a thought. That's how blind my faith was in my becoming a professional cricketer, and making a living out of it. My father had a lot to do with this.

He always thought I was a special talent. He would keep telling his friends I was even better than he was. He was certain I was going to play for India and this belief of his was etched deeply into my psyche. He never offered any criticism about my game, not even a word. Perhaps he didn't watch me closely enough to know my faults. I was told there was this one school game where he had sat down to watch me bat, and had suddenly set off to fetch one of his contemporaries to come see me. For the record, that match was going on in Azad Maidan while his friend was in Dadar – it was going to take him at least ninety minutes going to and fro, but he still went. He had the confidence I'd still be batting when he got back. And I was.

Just to be clear, I never played to seek his approval. Nor did he put any pressure of living his dream for him. I chased my own dreams. Today I might carry some insecurities and anxieties because of that childhood, but I will never hold a grudge against him. He died early, aged fifty-two, and that was it. I moved on. Life has been good.

*

To my mother Rekha, duty was always more important than emotion. We, her children, often challenged – through words and sometimes through actions – this guiding life principle of hers but only now do I realize why she was that way. Having emotions is easy. You don't have to work towards them; they are just there. Doing your duty, however, as a son, as a husband, as a parent, as an employee, needs commitment and sacrifice. That's tougher than being emotional.

I am like my mother in many ways. Sometimes I have made decisions that felt right emotionally, but I don't usually let emotions come in the way of my duties. I have seen people fail in their important duties and fumble their way through life just because they let their emotions get the better of them. I feel sorry for such people, but I feel sorrier for those who depend on them.

During her last days, when my mother was in the hospital, I'd be right next to her. Whenever she would regain consciousness and I could speak to her, she'd say, 'Don't worry, Shonu, I will always pray for you.' I guess she knew her time had come. Every time I remember this moment I well up. Even now as I write this, I have tears in my eyes. Her death is an event in my life that I have not been able to come to terms with. I felt so sad for her as her life was winding up. She did not have much happiness in her life. She lived a tough life, swimming against the tide daily for many years.

My mother was born in Mangalore, one of six children, to a simple salaried worker. She lived the first eighteen years of her life there, finished her school and then moved to Mumbai to earn money for her family. She had to leave home soon after her matriculation.

In Mumbai, she worked as a typist in a small private firm, and would commute to south Mumbai every day from Dadar's

Shivaji Park, where she stayed as a paying guest with a family acquaintance. Shivaji Park, of course, was my father's domain. He instantly fell in love with this simple girl who would mind her own business as she went to work every day, walking the streets of Mumbai with her head down.

My father and mother were extreme opposites. He was a loafer of sorts – street-smart, spoke the language of the street and was known for risqué humour. My mother was a simple south Indian woman who wore a sari to work. She was always well-groomed, not to look pretty but to look neat and clean. Not once did she ever utter a cuss word. She could not understand my father's humour, which was a big part of him. Vijay Manjrekar's humour was legendary in Mumbai's cricket circles, and here was his wife who responded with a blank expression whenever he cracked a joke. Perhaps that's what my father liked about her: She was different.

My father was a romantic but my mother was a pragmatist. She went to Mangalore to be with her parents for the delivery of each of her three kids. During those periods my father would often land at her doorstep to surprise her, but this would upset her – she hated surprises. They came in the way of her daily routine, her meticulous planning and her structured life.

Although they had a love marriage, their incompatibility made married life difficult. We knew that my father, with his problems post retirement, was not going to be an easy man to live with for any woman. But my mother pulled along admirably. She said she had to do her duty as 'a Hindu wife' – that's what she would keep saying, 'I am a Hindu wife.' I later learnt that her interpretation and understanding of religion was a bit different from everyone else's. I don't think she had a clear grasp of the concept. I have no such confusions, though. Religion has no place in my life. I feel it's an outdated concept.

My mother adhered to her version of religion, which was mostly idol worship, and she encouraged us to do the same. I was a sceptic – as most children are – and asked her uncomfortable questions about God. Since she struggled to offer any convincing explanations, my faith in such matters started fading out quite early in my life.

Post retirement, when my father lost direction in life, he stopped going to his nine-to-five job and soon we were struggling to make ends meet.

So my mother took matters in her own hands. She started working as a typist again, at the age of forty-five, in a factory owned by Vijay Merchant, who was kind enough to give her employment after learning of our plight. After a few months in that job, she began learning shorthand by taking a class after office hours. Her efforts at enhancing her skills paid off as she soon moved from being a typist to a stenographer and therefore got paid more as the bosses preferred someone who could quickly take down their drafts and type out letters and memos in minutes.

It was necessary for her that all her kids be educated. That was another duty she wanted to fulfil. That is why she would keep steering me towards my studies even when I was doing well as a cricketer. She wanted me to at least be a graduate. I'd get angry whenever she would ask me to focus on my studies and get a nice job. I used to wonder why she didn't realize the importance of all the runs that I put on the board. I didn't know then that she had already seen the man of the house put runs on the board and little else.

Once when we had gone to watch a match at the Wankhede Stadium, we bumped into a senior cricketing colleague of my father; he casually remarked that I must work harder and make some progress quickly as a junior cricketer. 'Look where Maninder Singh, Chetan Sharma, Sivaramakrishnan have already reached,' he said. And he left. A frown appeared on my mother's face. She said to me, 'It's okay if you want to quit this and focus on academics.'

I was livid when she suggested that. I left her there and walked home all the way from the Wankhede Stadium.

Becoming a Test cricketer was my dream, the only one I had. How could she have doubts about me achieving it?

When I played for India, she would proudly introduce me to her friends and family as her 'Test-cricketer son'. I would then tease her about how she wanted me to quit cricket. She would just smile. Again, it was the insecurity in her about making ends meet, pursuing academics and getting a job. That was a safer route to stability in life, wasn't it?

Despite all her travails, I think she liked being the wife of the famous Vijay Manjrekar and then the mother of another Test cricketer. She enjoyed the attention she received.

It was her brother, Ramesh, younger to her by a couple of years, who was her real support. She once told me how he, barely out of his twenties, had come to meet my father to tell him that if their marriage was not working he was happy to take his sister home with him, and that he would rather see her separated than be miserable. My father therefore knew early in his marriage that he had a brother-in-law that could not be messed with.

I, too, have great regard for Ramesh uncle, who, like my mother, always put duty first. For years he was the guardian of all those from his extended family who travelled from Mangalore to Mumbai for a living. All of them stayed with him first before moving out when they got jobs. He had a family – a wife and three boys – to look after, but as a guardian it was his duty to look after all those who came from his native place. It didn't matter that his house was quite small. For him, like it was for my mother, it was all about doing the right thing.

My mother managed to raise her kids well. Once her duties as mother and wife were over, her focus turned to her house: Moonreach. She used to say it was a house left for her by her husband, and that it was her duty to look after it. It was as if her husband had left behind a treasure chest that she had to keep safe. She would take her obsession to extreme levels sometimes. Many a time, she would not come out with us because she could not keep the house locked. There had to be someone in the house all the time.

Her house was her occupation in her old age, a mission, a motivation to wake up every morning. As my family started growing, I moved out to a bigger house, which was not too far from her. She refused to move with me. After this, what made her happiest was her children visiting her for a meal in her Moonreach. She loved cooking. The monthly pension of Rs 35,000 that she received from the BCCI as the widow of a Test cricketer meant she did not have to depend on her children for money now. Her last days were peaceful, living in her own house and on her own terms.

*

My father had one rare quality that eluded other retired cricketers. He was never envious of successive generations of cricketers for the wonderful life they were leading. Cricketers in India invariably become bigger stars and live a richer life than those of yesteryears. That is a life the retired cricketers came close to having – it's no surprise that they often end up feeling a bit resentful.

On the contrary, my father loved having current cricketers over at home for lunches and dinners. When the players came to our house, I would become the 'umbrella man'. Being an umbrella man involved waiting outside our house near the main road, Gokhale Road in Dadar, with an umbrella in hand. When these cricketers would arrive, I would then hold an umbrella over them in such a way that the public could not see their faces. They were not supposed to know that India's cricket stars were here. For that would attract a big crowd, and my father did not want that.

I am proud to say that even before I turned eleven, I had been an umbrella man to several Test cricketers, including Sunil Gavaskar, Gundappa Viswanath, Bhagwath Chandrasekhar and Erapalli Prasanna. Come to think of it, the umbrella didn't serve any purpose: At my height, I was never able to completely cover them and shield their faces from the public. On the contrary the act seemed to attract even more attention to them.

That home on Gokhale Road in Dadar, called Krishna Kamal, was a modest house, but the who's who of the cricketing world have been there, including the great West Indian, Rohan Kanhai. We lived there as a joint family. My grandfather, my father's father, lay on a sick bed in the drawing room, right at the entrance of the flat. We used to call him 'dada'. He was paralysed and bedridden and remained in that state for thirteen years before he died. How my grandmother diligently looked after him for all those years was an early lesson in loyalty and devotion.

Whenever we had celebrity guests over, curtains would be drawn around my grandfather's bed so that the guests didn't feel awkward seeing him. They would be taken straight to our bedroom, a small room in the house. For such occasions, we would decorate the house with brand new curtains, hung on all windows. As kids we would be thrilled to bits. First, because of the kind of guests that were visiting and second because of how much better our house would look.

My mother, though, was always ashamed of this house, especially when guests came over. To her the washing area was so bad that she would insist on offering a big aluminium bowl to the guests in the bedroom to wash their hands after they had eaten. My father was quite unperturbed by such things. He was just excited and happy to have the cricketers over. One of the happiest days of my mother's life was when we finally moved out of Krishna Kamal into our new house.

The visits of these great stars to our old house were a source of great inspiration for a seven-year-old boy who had set his sights on becoming a cricketer. Not just Test cricketers; even when club cricketers from the famous Shivaji Park Gymkhana Club team came home I would be over the moon. Especially when they came for a quick meal during the lunch break of a match because then they would be in their whites. Or rather their creams: Cricketers preferred their whites to be off-white for some reason.

I was always fascinated by those off-whites – the fall of their trousers, the pleats on them – some had one pleat, others two – the rolled-up sleeves up to the elbows. I craved to wear those clothes. Since I was not a very demanding child – at least I think so – I didn't pester anyone to buy me a set of cricket clothes. Eventually when I got my first whites, I got them as a matter of my right. I got selected to play for my school team at the age of twelve, so I needed cricketing whites. The cloth was bought from a factory outlet at Laxmi Vishnu Mills. I insisted it be off-white. Once it was sent for tailoring I counted the days. The day the 'whites' finally arrived was one of the happiest days of my life. My trousers had two pleats.

The sound of spiked cricket boots gave me goosebumps as a child. It was captivating every time they came in contact with stone flooring. It all started when I began watching matches at Shivaji Park Gymkhana. I used to see the players return to the pavilion from the ground. The spikes that were silent on the turf would suddenly come to life when they hit the hard floor of the pavilion. I just loved that clanky, metallic, rhythmic sound the cricketers made with their spiked boots as they would tread carefully on the smooth, hard floor. It was like music to my ears. I would, on occasion, secretly wear my father's big, spiked boots and walk around our room in them. I felt just like a Test cricketer wearing them.

If my father had learnt what I had been up to, he would not have been happy. Vijay Manjrekar was renowned in the cricketing circles for the way he took care of his cricket gear. They were like little idols of worship for him.

The other thing about cricket that I first fell in love with was the flap of the pad above the knee roll, how it would go back and forth when a batsman walked. It would fascinate me. It was something that I would watch most when at the cricket ground. Not the batsman's strokes, not the bowling, not the fielding, but the flaps of the batsman's pads going back and forth. When I had my first set of pads, I was so caught up in their flaps' movement that I worried they would distract me from watching the ball.

As a father, today when I think of it, it's quite amazing, the things that can consume a child's mind. An adult can never truly fathom that, even if he or she was a child once.

2

THE WONDER YEARS

I MIGHT NOT have taken my father to my matches, but he used to take me to his during my school breaks. If not for those visits to Shivaji Park Gymkhana, it is quite possible I might not have become a cricketer. However, it wasn't what I saw on the field that got me – it was what happened around the field.

In fact, I hardly watched the cricketing action on the field. Instead, I'd be found playing in the corner of the ground by myself or with players who were not in the playing eleven, who were happy to indulge the son of the great Vijay Manjrekar. After the game, my father would come around to ask me whether I liked a certain shot he had played. I would lie – 'I liked it very much.'

So I looked forward to my visits to the Shivaji Park Gymkhana despite not being a great fan of watching cricket. The bhelpuri that Gopal's Canteen served there was unique. Invariably one of the players would offer me a cold drink. They'd ask me which one I preferred, Coca Cola, Mangola or Gold Spot, but I was happy to have any of them. Soft drinks were a rare treat.

During the Kanga League, sometimes the Shivaji Park team would go for lunch to Sanmaan, a nearby restaurant which served vegetarian snacks. The day the team decided they would eat at Sanmaan, I'd start drooling for their burger, considered the star item on the menu.

The Shivaji Park Gymkhana cricket team was a star-studded one, with a few Test players in it, but they weren't afraid to walk the streets in their whites to go together to nearby restaurants to eat. There would always be a crowd of cricket fans who'd follow them all the way to the restaurants and back, but it was no big deal for the players. When I think of those days, I find it amusing how today's cricket stars are whisked away by their personal security teams. Increasingly I find cricketing celebrities behaving and being treated like film stars. I am not sure I like this trend.

I used to be proud about the fact that despite their fame, cricketers would continue to behave like regular middle-class people. Once you make this a habit, life after retirement becomes easier. (Rahul Dravid is a great example of this.) However, I must confess that it was this fame, this adulation, the fact that people on the street on a working day would follow my father and his team to a restaurant that made me want to be a cricketer in the first place. At a young age, I had my first brush with fame through my father and his celebrity guests. After all, I had held umbrellas for them. I knew I wanted to be like them.

*

I was one of those privileged kids who could get to see their heroes in flesh and blood. My hero was Sunil Gavaskar. I think I inherited this admiration from my father. He used to take every opportunity to meet Gavaskar. My father was like a brother to Gavaskar's mother. Every Raksha Bandhan my father would go to their house and I'd go along too.

There's an interesting memory associated with him. I was once at a match at the Cross Maidan in south Mumbai when a kid came up to our tent asking for me. He said, 'Sunil Gavaskar is looking for you and he is waiting there.' He pointed to a tree just outside the ground.

At first I didn't believe him, but when I saw where he was pointing, the great Sunil Gavaskar was indeed standing there under a tree. Mind you, this was sometime around the year 1980, and at that time, Gavaskar was the most famous Indian personality, in the same league as Bollywood superstar Amitabh Bachchan. Also, he was my cricket idol, the man I worshipped and often copied in my batting.

When I walked up to him, Gavaskar was holding a brand-new harrow-sized Gray-Nicolls bat in his hand. He said that my father had asked him to get one for me from England. Along with the bat, he also handed me a rolled-up poster of a Gray-Nicolls advertisement where Greg Chappell is seen with a streaker with a Gray-Nicolls bat.

I remember not walking back to my tent. I must have glided. Everybody could see what had happened. They looked at me in awe when I returned with the bat.

Not only was I ecstatic at having received the bat, I was also touched that Gavaskar had personally come to present it to me. He was a busy man and he could have easily got that bat delivered to me through somebody, but he chose to present it to me himself, taking the trouble to find out where I was playing and then making that journey.

He truly knew the meaning of such gestures. I remember when he wrote a special letter to Sachin Tendulkar when he did not get the best junior cricketer award. It was remarkable for a player in his position to first know about this small fact and then feel so strongly about it that he sat and penned the letter.

From the time he was young, Gavaskar was fond of writing. As a cricketer, he would reply to every fan letter he would get. He even wrote to me – on my father's request, of course – a letter after his life-changing 1971 West Indies tour. He must have been twenty-one then.

Because I am a commentator now, I get to spend a lot of time with people like him, and greats like Ian Chappell, Wasim Akram and even Vivian Richards. We work, eat and drink together like friends, but I never let myself forget how lucky I am to be in their close circle.

*

Apart from letting me get a sneak peek of the fame associated with cricket, the other significant thing my father did was move houses when I was about ten years old. Living in Dadar, I grew up in the world of cricket, but in our old house, my exposure to cricket was limited. The little space between two buildings was our cricket ground. We played with soft balls until our mothers shouted from the house windows that dinner was ready.

Our move to a two-bedroom apartment in Prabhadevi, to a complex called Moonreach, was the first significant step to shape Sanjay Manjrekar the cricketer. My father bought it with the money he got from his benefit match held in Hubli in the early 1970s. (Benefit matches were a wonderful concept. They recognized that cricketers were not worldly wise, and that they needed a bit of a financial support now that they were entering the mainstream after retirement. Thankfully cricketers these days are smarter with their finances.)

This apartment in Moonreach – named so because it was the tallest building in the area, all of thirteen floors – cost us Rs 78,000 then. It is worth crores now. I grew up to be a Test cricketer in this building. My life as a Test cricketer ended while we stayed there, but more on that later.

I had more young boys to play cricket with at Moonreach. Relatively speaking, if there were six boys who'd played near our old house, now there were fifteen in our apartment complex. Also, there was more space for us to play. Those were fun days, and I made some really good friends there. Luckily, all of them were decent cricketers, so my game was properly honed. At one point of time, the complex saw three young boys play soft-ball cricket together with me – Sanjay Pednekar, Subhash Kshirsagar and Raju Kulkarni. They went on to play for Mumbai's Under-19 team, the Ranji Trophy and the Indian national team respectively.

Even in that little area in our premises, when we would play our under-arm cricket with soft ball mostly for fun, I batted like my life depended on it. I would just keep defending and not play attacking shots. One day, after they had spent a lot of time trying to get me out, my close friend Sanjay Pednekar got so furious that he walked away from the game and didn't talk to me for days. He found my obsession with defence infuriating. 'Have some fun, man!' he said. 'Play some shots, take some risks.'

Basically, he wanted me to give the bowlers a chance to get me out, but that is what I always wanted to deny them as a batsman. I loved batting defensively. That was my natural game, and my real strength. Even when I played table tennis, I seemed to lose points when I played attacking shots. I won matches by frustrating opponents by returning everything.

Sadly, the common area in that complex where we played cricket for hours on end, where we unwittingly developed our games, is now a parking lot. Moonreach doesn't produce cricketers any more. Academies could not have replicated the training I got as a cricketer in that compound of ours.

I played the game only because I thought I was destined to play for India; my father had drilled that thought into my head by introducing me to others as a future Test cricketer, telling me how I was better than he was at my age. Moving towards domestic – and then national and international – cricket was the natural step. Growing up in Mumbai, I didn't have to fumble my way through. There was a roadmap in front of me. The first step was school cricket, and our school, IES English Medium School, took its cricket seriously.

Funnily, this was an English school that made my Marathi stronger because English was used only for written communication. It may seem strange to hear this today, but speaking English confidently was a challenge for me for years, especially when I came in contact with students from other proper English schools or English colleges. I remember when we moved about in such groups, I would remain silent for long, framing and rehearsing some sentence in English in my head. Then I would utter that sentence, an act which would bring immediate relief because now I could be quiet for a while!

My father had no such issues with English. He once wrote a letter to my principal at IES. Its contents were sharp and to the point, conveying to my school that his son, Vijay Manjrekar's son, should be given a chance to play in the school cricket team. He, too, believed I was always going to play for India. Perhaps he felt he was doing the school a favour by offering my services.

On receipt of the letter, I immediately got an invitation to join the school nets. H.S. Bhor, the physical training (PT) teacher who was also in charge of the cricket team, conducted the nets. After a few days of net practice, I was chosen to play in a friendly match. I failed badly – not once but twice. I was out of my depth playing with hard ball and with all the equipment on. I was so embarrassed by my own performance that after those two matches I stopped going to the school nets. My absence went unnoticed; it was no big deal, I hadn't done anything for them to miss me. Maybe the school authorities were just happy that the 'son of the Test cricketer' had been put in his place.

A few months later, I got a chance to practise with the Air India cricket team at the Shivaji Park Gymkhana grounds. My father was a proud employee of the airline for a number of years. He had a sticker on his car window that said 'I am an Air Indian'. In those two months at the Air India nets, I got a pretty good idea how to bat against the hard ball, and in full gear. My father had instructed the Air India players not to bowl any differently to me just because I was eleven years old. In those two months, I got some real training of playing hard-ball cricket.

The following year, I entered the school team through the open selection trials held in our school grounds where hundreds attended. Bhor told me later that I looked like a completely different player this time. That was the beginning of three good years of school cricket for IES. Under my captaincy, we won the famous Giles Shield tournament for the first time.

Those days of Giles Shield cricket were some of the best days of my life. We lived to see our names in the newspaper next day. If you got a century in any match, there was a good chance you would be featured in the sports pages. It was a great thrill for an eleven-year-old to see his name in a mainstream daily. I would spend restless nights in sheer excitement before those games because I would visualize getting a hundred and seeing my name in the newspapers.

There used to be this sports reporter – a stringer – who would make the rounds of cricket grounds collecting scores of teams. He might have been doing the most basic job for newspapers, but for us he was an important man, a VIP – after all, our names making it to the sports pages depended on him. If he missed your match, did you *really* score a century? So when one of us did reach a hundred, we'd have one eye towards the tent, eyes scanning to find him even as you went about your innings. What a joy it would be to spot him – the old, hunched, slow-moving figure, our ticket to fame.

After one of my Giles Shield hundreds, the umpire for that game told me to take my photograph to the *Times of India* office. I was not sure, but he seemed keen and pestered me to do it. After the game, I boarded a BEST bus from south Bombay to Prabhadevi, my residence, picked up my black-and-white passport-size photo, and travelled all the way back to the *Times of India* office. The umpire accompanied me, and showed me where the sports desk was, and made sure I handed over the photo to the right person. It was worth the effort: My photograph appeared in the sports pages the next day.

The umpire was Vijay Gaundalkar, a famous personality in Mumbai cricket. Everyone in Mumbai's cricket scene knew him. He was from a well-educated family and was himself a learned person, but being a cricket lover he took to umpiring. However, his love for the game got the better of him – he started to lose his mind, and there was a time he even roamed the streets of Mumbai like a beggar. Towards the end of my career, I once saw him being shooed away when he tried to approach us players at a cricket ground. He was being ridiculed and ostracized for his exceptional love and unparalleled passion for cricket.

When I am around, though, I make sure no one touches him. He has as much right to be at a cricket ground as we cricketers do. Like my father, Gaundalkar, too, devoted his life to cricket. For all the celebrity and fame the sport can bring you, it is not easy to be so devoted to it.

*

> *'If I have a date with Madhuri Dixit and a friend calls me and says he wants to meet me, I will happily cancel my date with Madhuri.'*

These words pretty much tell you everything you need to know about Sanjay Pednekar, my next-door neighbour, and a unique friend who greatly affected my teen life and left some extraordinary memories that will stay with me forever. He was one of the three – apart from me – boys at Moonreach who went on to play representative cricket.

Sanju died of bone cancer at the age of thirty-six. When he breathed his last in the hospital, it came upon me to tell his mother and father that their son had died. He came from a jewellers' family, and he too went into the jewellery business early in his adult life. Perhaps he knew all along he would have to get into the family business at some point; he lived his teen life to the fullest.

Since the first time I met him – I was twelve and he sixteen – Sanju always had cash in his pocket, and he spent it all on his friends. Naturally, he had a large circle of friends. He was ahead of his time in everything. Before we had even heard of an electronic gadget he would already have it in his possession. His family was not highly educated, but he was into healthy living – balanced diet, exercising and strength training. Before cancer took him away, he had made long-term plans for his wife and son to grow up in Australia. He felt that his son would have a better life there.

Sanju played for Sharadashram Vidyamandir, the same school as Sachin Tendulkar. He went on to play for Mumbai Under-19, and I was thrilled for him. The day he was selected, he treated me to dinner at the Nanking Chinese restaurant, a few hundred metres from the Wankhede Stadium, the venue of the selection trials. At the age of fifteen, a meal at Nanking for someone like me was a huge deal and he kept giving us such exotic treats for years. Sometimes I'd feel a bit guilty and embarrassed that he always paid for my meals at fancy restaurants, whereas I could not even offer to pay him because I just couldn't afford it. At one stage I began to humbly decline his invitations. Sensing my predicament, it was he who came up with the suggestion that I could pay once I started earning.

When I got my first pay cheque, I proudly treated Sanju to a Chinese meal at Flora restaurant in Worli – my father used to treat the family here sometimes. Sanju was awkward right through the meal because I was going to pay for us. Once, after practice, we saw an acquaintance while waiting in a queue for a bus near Metro Cinema in south Mumbai. Suddenly Sanju tensed up. I asked him why, and he said, 'I don't have enough money to pay for his bus ticket.' I don't know what it was with him, but he felt he had an obligation to pay for others all the time.

Even now, when we friends meet – all whose lives Sanju touched in one way or the other – it's impossible not to talk about him. He had a great sense of humour, and we remember his legendary one-liners. Whenever you told him you were going out, he had comments ready for the place you were going to visit. It could be any place, but Sanju had visited them all, and knew their faults. If you were going to Neelam restaurant, he would ask you to carry a rodent trap. For the bar at Sea Rock Hotel in Bandra, he would recommend carrying your own blanket.

For another restaurant, he would recommend carrying a flash light. This was a place where he had been annoyed by a man laughing next to him, but only later did he realize it was his own reflection in the mirror. The place was just too dimly lit for him to see that.

Sanju was not great at spoken English, but for some reason the waiters at all these restaurants and bars spoke only in English. So Sanju would rattle out his order – he had memorized what to eat where – and would only respond with a 'yeah' if the waiters had any follow-up questions.

He was one of the first to have a VCR (video cassette recorder) on which we used to watch tapes of cricket matches from Channel 9 and English movies. We used to rent VHS (video home system) tapes from a movie library, and their boy at the counter would always struggle to pronounce the names of available titles. His own English notwithstanding, once Sanju told him, 'Why don't you film yourself speaking all these names? I would rent that video at double the price.'

Sanju had a special set of friends with whom he went out with only at night. Not once did he push me to join him on these night escapades. Some of those boys did drugs, some others got up to other serious mischief. Sanju wanted to protect me from all that. He wanted me to play for India more badly than I did. He felt those night-outs were not good for me, a boy with dreams of playing for India. I owe him eternal gratitude for that.

*

Before going on to fulfil Sanju's and my wish, though, I experienced what almost all Indian cricketers had to go through at that time. I was selected to captain the Mumbai University team for a month-long tournament in Baroda, all expenses paid for by the university. So the seventeen of us, the best college-level cricketers in Mumbai, travelled to Baroda by train, unreserved, in second-class compartments. Once there, we were shown to our three bare rooms in the MS University hostel. Sure, the rooms had four walls and a ceiling each, but there was nothing in between. The common washroom was outside the rooms, down the corridor. This was to be our home for a month.

The first thing we did when we 'checked in' was tie a string diagonally across the room; this way we'd utilize the maximum length of the rope, and therefore have more space to hang our clothes. Not the wet ones – the rope was to be our wardrobe. We were carrying our bed rolls – sleeping bags – which on university tours like these were about as necessary as cricket kitbags.

We had Rs 25 each as daily allowance. Together, we cut a deal with a tea shop nearby to supply us our morning and afternoon tea with naan khatais, the local name for cookies. Dinner for my six room-mates used to be three palak paneers, three aloo gobhis and three dals with rotis from Gayatri Bhavan, a budget restaurant near

Baroda railway station. For dessert, we'd order three lassis [yoghurt smoothies]. Almighty fights would break out with accusations flying about that the person drinking first drank more than half of it.

While playing that tournament, the Rohinton Baria Inter-varsity Trophy, we, in many ways, also subconsciously trained ourselves in living off the land, in armed forces parlance. Until one day when we got lucky. Mayank Khandwala, a left-arm spinner in our side, had his father visiting him, and we were all treated to a meal at a posh restaurant called Kontiki. I was not the only 'cricketer son' in that group. Dilip Sardesai's son, Rajdeep, was there with us too, and he stayed in the room next door. It was a significant trip for him too. He later told me that after seeing me get all those runs on that trip, he had realized what was needed to play for India, and he knew he had didn't have it in him. He chose journalism instead; I am so proud of what he has achieved in this field.

The Rohinton Baria Trophy was played on flat matting tracks. I found myself in great form, and scored six consecutive hundreds. I remember eavesdropping on a conversation that was happening in the tent next to us. The Delhi University team were having a team chat at tea time after I had just finished my sixth hundred. The fielders were complaining to the coach, 'Sir, he is not playing one dead defensive shot. Either he is pushing or driving for runs off the front foot or pushing or driving for runs off the back foot.'

Apart from that tournament, only twice in my career have I experienced such perfection with the bat. One, in 1989, against Pakistan in Pakistan, and then at a much lower level, in a domestic limited-overs inter-company tournament, the SAIL Trophy in 1996, where I almost single-handedly won all the matches for my team. Now when I think about those performances, I can recollect only how I felt during those phases, not the nuances, not how I played certain shots.

Maybe it's because you tend to remember struggles more vividly than the flawless patches of your career. I remember not what I was doing right in Baroda but the camaraderie. The wonderful thing about college cricket is, when you are playing well the others are willing you to do well. Not everyone plays with ambitions of playing for India, so they are genuinely happy to see someone else do well. I felt that support and goodwill of many players every step of the way during that one month in Baroda. However, at the highest level, everything is a bit cut-throat. You never get that kind of support from your team-mates at the international level.

*

As a college cricketer, I used to be quite pleased with my game until one day a team member and friend, Salil Datar, brought his father to the nets – he was going to film our batting. Later that day, we assembled at the Datars. I was excited at the prospect of watching myself bat for the first time. But I didn't like what I saw – it was underwhelming. In hindsight, that was the day the journey of the harsh analysis of my own game began.

As a commentator and as an expert, I am often quite critical of cricketers' performances. They must feel hurt when they hear it, but they don't know it is nothing compared to how much I criticize myself. After that evening at the Datars, the second time I saw myself on TV was when I saw a few shots of my batting in the news bulletin after I had scored a hundred for India Under-25 against the touring Pakistanis. It was a good innings against a really good international attack. A young and fiery Wasim Akram had terrorized the rest of the batsmen. What's more, my century was a critical innings since I was close to the Indian team's selection announcement. When I saw myself on TV driving Wasim off the front foot and later cutting Tauseef Ahmed, I didn't like what I saw.

Sachin Tendulkar used to tease me, calling me Mr Perfect and Mr Different. To some extent, he was right. Subconsciously that is what I sought to be. It is easy to be different, but as I found out over the course of my career, it is nearly impossible to be perfect. So I kept pursuing perfection. It frustrated me when I couldn't achieve it. Even if I scored a double-hundred, the very next day I'd be watching the telecast footage, trying to correct the two shots in that innings that I had not quite played right.

Before I went to Baroda for the Rohinton Baria Trophy, I was scoring only 30s and 40s, and that really troubled me. So I spoke to former Mumbai captain and stalwart Milind Rege before we left for the month-long tour. Rege gave me what I thought was pretty standard advice: 'You need to concentrate, Sanjay.'

Somewhat annoyed at the stock phrase, I asked him what exactly 'concentrating' was. 'How does one do it? What's the method?' I asked him.

Rege hadn't expected this follow-up question. Caught slightly off guard, he took his time, thought deeply and then defined carefully what he thought concentration meant: 'To play every ball as if your life depended on it is concentrating. "I will not get out to this ball" – that is what you must say before every ball you face, no matter how long you bat or how many balls you face.'

Finally, somebody had given the broad term 'concentrate' a specific shape. Maybe others define concentration differently but this definition worked perfectly for me. It was as if I had been given the key to a treasure chest. Now my 30s and 40s began turning into big hundreds. I got those six hundreds in Baroda, and a few days later I made my Ranji Trophy debut against Haryana.

*

Living on shared smoothies and teas, I might have scored six hundreds in six matches in the Rohinton Baria Trophy in Baroda, but I wonder if it would have been possible without the life-changing experience I had in Muscat a year earlier. The year was 1983, I was eighteen years old and was on my first trip outside India. Ajit Wadekar had organized a fundraiser cricket match, part of whose proceeds were to come to us, the late Vijay Manjrekar's family. My father had died a few months earlier, and Wadekar was aware we weren't doing well financially.

This was a match between a full-strength Indian team and an almost full-strength England side. Because I was a cricketer of some repute at junior levels, I was allowed to play as a member of that Indian squad – it was the same side which had just won the World Cup. For two days, I travelled, dined and even shopped with them. Wherever the Indian team went, people assumed I was an India player too.

This was my first experience of what being an Indian team cricketer meant – it was like being a film star. People just wanted to pamper you all the time. My ambition of wanting to be a Test player got reinforced during this tour, but soon that ambition would be shattered. A rude awakening awaited me.

Starting with my father and his friends, every cricketer I knew was a Test cricketer. Almost all the male adults I had known outside my family and school were Test cricketers. Until then,

I had thought it was my right to smoothly progress to play Test cricket. Either my father was obsessed about turning me into a Test batsman, or he'd seen genuine potential in me, but unwittingly he had brainwashed me into believing I was going to play for India. This process began when I was nine.

So there I was, the eighteen-year-old cocky son of a former Test cricketer, walking out to bat at No. 7 in the Vijay Manjrekar memorial match in Muscat. I could hear and see the laughter and banter among the players as I took guard. This was a casual match, but I was up against established international bowlers.

Mike Hendrick came off a short run-up, and I am still taken aback by the pace I'd felt on that first ball. It was something I had never experienced before. I made a mental note of the speed in the air and got ready to face the next ball. It was a yorker. Before I could get my bat down, it had hit the stumps behind me. I, future Test batsman, was bowled second ball to a bowler who was well past his prime and was bowling off a short run-up in an exhibition match.

This was brutal. I sat by myself in a corner and sobbed. In what was a casual, exhibition-match atmosphere, everybody thought I overreacted. I was okay after a while but I had got a taste of what was in store. I still wanted to *be* a cricket star – I had been in those shoes and loved every minute of it – but I knew now that I needed to work bloody hard on my game. That day was the first time I doubted if I would play for India.

I went back, worked on my game. A year later I made those six university hundreds, and the dream was back on track. I played for Mumbai in 1985, and in 1987, against West Indies in foggy weather in Delhi, I got my Test debut before I expected. I thought there were a couple of batsmen ahead of me in the queue, but this was an early lesson that when the West Indies team was in town, injuries made convenient appearances.

I got my blue woollen classic India cap the night before the Test. I wore it, and stood in front of the mirror, admiring myself. I felt I had accomplished everything. That I had achieved my goal. I did not care or worry about how many runs I was going to get in the match. Just seeing that crest on the blue cap was thrilling. I had seen that logo everywhere, and envied people who had it on their shirts, their caps, their kitbags. Now I was one of them. I was an India Test cricketer.

3

THE MUMBAI SCHOOL OF BATTING

RUNS AT THE right time are more crucial than aggregate runs. This timing is just as important as meeting the ball under your nose. I know a few batsmen who didn't play for India just because they failed when it all mattered: the big week just before the selection. The first week of 1987, I thought, could have been one such week for me. I had already played one Test – scoring 5 and 10 as West Indies pulverized us for 75 and 327 in Delhi – but was going to miss the Tests against Sri Lanka.

Pakistan were due to visit India later that season, and I was hoping to score some timely runs just before selection for those Tests, when I travelled back to the scene of my forgettable Test debut, Delhi, for a Deodhar Trophy match. The Deodhar Trophy was the one-day version of Duleep Trophy, an inter-zonal tournament played between five teams comprising of the best players of the respective zones. This was only my third List A match.

Anshuman Gaekwad, our West Zone captain, and Shrikant Kalyani from Maharashtra had a long partnership for the third wicket. We were reaching a time when all that the remaining batsmen could do was go and hit out. If they got a chance to bat, that is. As the partnership grew, the feeling inside me kept growing that if I got to bat then it would be a nothing-to-gain and all-to-lose situation. If I scored a quick 30, no one would notice. If I got out for a single-digit score playing a big shot, it would be a failure from a selection candidate.

Feeling uneasy about this, I went up to Lalchand Rajput, a senior team-mate from Mumbai who had opened the innings. Rajput played two Tests for India, but was more importantly the coach when they won the World T20 in 2007 and when they won the triangular ODI series in Australia a year later. He was a respected member of the team. With trepidation, I explained myself to Rajput, and asked if it was okay if I didn't bat in my assigned position.

Rajput said it was okay, but the look he gave me while saying so left nothing to imagination: That look made sure I realized what I was asking for. It was a look from a cricketer who thought the other cricketer was being selfish and cowardly, but equally it was a look from a Mumbai cricketer to another Mumbai cricketer. It told me that the way I was thinking was not in keeping with the spirit of Mumbai cricket.

I felt sheepish and relieved at the same time when he said yes. The relief was short-lived because we collapsed, and I had to go in to bat at No. 10 where I ended up scoring a duck. We lost the match easily, to our bitter rivals – North Zone. Cricket had served instant justice. However, considering the ease with which Manoj Prabhakar and Surinder Khanna chased down our 206 in under

40 overs, I doubt if my batting at my original position would have made much of a difference.

This was a low-key match. Not much was reported in newspapers. I hoped no one would notice, and went back to preparing for the rest of the Ranji Trophy season. Our next assignment was the quarter-final against Karnataka. In the lead-up to the match, all Mumbai cricketers began practising at Wankhede Stadium. Ravi Shastri and Dilip Vengsarkar, both India Test stars, also joined us at the nets. We were due to travel to Bangalore, while they were scheduled to go to Faridabad for a warm-up game against the Pakistan team before the first Test against them on 23 January 1987 in Madras.

Shastri was bowling his left-arm spin to me in an open-wicket session. Everything was normal. Then I stepped out and hit him over the covers, straight onto the wooden benches of the famous East Stand of the Wankhede Stadium.

I could not believe what happened next. Shastri strode angrily towards me, and asked me, 'Why couldn't you go in to bat in that Deodhar game and hit like that?'

I was shocked. During my Deodhar Trophy game, Shastri was in Cuttack to play against Sri Lanka in a Test match. I thought to myself: 'How did this guy, who had been away from that game, which was not even reported about in the newspapers, come to know about this, and also feel so strongly about it?'

That's when I understood that a Mumbai batsman chickening out of a tight situation was big news among Mumbai cricketers. The famous grapevine of Mumbai cricket ensured that this kind of gossip spread too. You could earn yourself a reputation in no time. I felt very small when Shastri confronted me that day. Later, he explained to me calmly why I should not be thinking the way I did.

I learnt my lesson that day. After that episode, not once in my cricketing life have I avoided a tough situation. What turned out to be my last Test innings came as an opener against Allan Donald, Fanie de Villiers and Brian McMillan. My confidence at that stage was at rock bottom but in a desperate bid to extend my Test career I backed myself to open the innings. I have seen Indian openers get mysterious injuries seeing the fast-bowling attack of the opposition, but here I was, a middle-order batsman, down on confidence, going up the order to face the new ball against South Africa.

I scored 34 and 5 in the two innings before Javagal Srinath won us that Test. I never played for India again, but I know Mumbai cricket will be proud of me because they didn't care about failure much if you didn't shirk a challenge. In a way, without meaning to do so, I exited Test cricket in true Mumbai fashion.

*

'After you get to fifty, go for a hundred. After the hundred, look for 150. Then double-hundred…'

In Mumbai, batting milestones were just that – milestones, and not the destination. This fundamental thought of batting was drilled into every young Mumbai batsman starting from the school level at the age of eleven. Batsmen who didn't get big scores, who threw their wicket away after a fifty or even a hundred, were treated like outcasts. Mumbai didn't care for them. It didn't invest its time and energy in such players.

Sunil Gavaskar and others like him were the role models at that time. Batsmen who got big hundreds, batsmen who never gave their wickets away. When I was seventeen, I saw a senior Mumbai cricket figure being furious with Vengsarkar for scoring 'only' 123 in the 1983-84 Ranji final when Gavaskar went on to convert his hundred into a double and stayed not out.

The term *khadoos* has come to be ridiculed a bit, partly because of its overuse, but that is exactly what we were asked to be. To not give our wicket away, come what may. 'When you reach a hundred, take a fresh guard and bat as if starting a new innings,' we were taught. There were batsmen who not only used to take that fresh guard, they used to make sure everybody noticed it too. To tell the opposition they weren't done with them yet. To show it to their coaches they were being *khadoos*.

The seniors encouraged you to be *khadoos* but they were, in fact, generous people. The backbone of Mumbai cricket was these generous seniors – former cricketers, umpires, selectors or just Mumbai's cricket fans – who would go to various maidans only to watch young exciting talent and try to facilitate their growth. These cricket people found joy not in match results but in spotting future India players.

It didn't matter to this community where the talent came from: which school or college, what his surname was or which part of India his family came from. They would share their discoveries with everyone they met. Wasim Jaffer, and now Armaan Jaffer, will never feel prejudiced in this city. Vinod Kambli would have struggled to get a break so easily for any other state. Mumbai looked past earrings and his rapper-like clothes. Mumbai picked him when he was ready to play for Mumbai. Nothing else mattered.

As Mumbai captain, I remember sitting in on a selection meeting at the start of a new season. Wasim Jaffer's name came up for discussion. I had only heard of Wasim; I listened to what the other selectors had to say. Most of them were pressing for his selection in the Ranji squad. Wasim was just eighteen then, and hence eligible to play for Mumbai's Under-19 too. One of the selectors, who was also chairman of the Under-19 selection committee, pleaded to the others to keep him at the Under-19 level. This would make the Under-19 team very strong, he said. This is when I intervened: 'Is he good enough to play for the Mumbai Ranji team? If he is, we should pick him and not worry about Under-19.'

Now, every selector had to dig deep inside and answer an honest cricketing question: Under-19 or Ranji?

They all said Ranji.

Each of the selectors was a Mumbai stalwart, part of the community of Mumbai cricket people. It was this community that had identified Sachin Tendulkar as the next big thing when he was twelve years old. As India players, we took pride in knowing there were the likes of Tendulkar and Kambli in the supply chain to the extent that during an ODI against New Zealand in Baroda, in 1988, Vengsarkar began to wind Kapil Dev up. 'There's another *ghoda* [thoroughbred] coming from Mumbai, Sachin Tendulkar,' Vengsarkar told Kapil, a North Zone rival. 'You know, he's just thirteen or fourteen but what a superb player he is. So watch out.'

During that conversation, Vengsarkar arranged a now-famous net session at the Brabourne Stadium in Mumbai where Kapil bowled to Tendulkar even before he had played for Mumbai. This was during a training camp before the West Indies tour. Vengsarkar told Tendulkar – then just a school kid – to 'just come and bat in the India nets'. He played Kapil effortlessly, but the attitude of a Mumbai senior promoting talent is worthy of praise here.

There is evidence to suggest they didn't limit this generosity to Mumbai talent. In 1997 we played our Wills Trophy knockout matches in Punjab: one in Jalandhar, two in Mohali. Kambli at that time was at his peak, and he used to just murder spin bowling. In the nets, a local off-spinner, a sixteen-year-old scrawny little sardar, bowled to Kambli, and every time he tried to hit, the ball just went straight up. As soon as the net session got over, our coach, Balwinder Sandhu, took this young sardar lad to a corner, and offered him to come to Mumbai. Although he didn't accept the offer, within six months the sardarji, Harbhajan Singh, made his debut for Punjab and within a year he was playing for India.

In November 1996, as I waited my turn to bat in the nets just before the Titan Cup final at Wankhede Stadium, I saw a left-arm quick, a local nets bowler, trouble Mohammad Azharuddin a bit. Anything Azhar would do, the ball seemed to hit him on the pads before his bat could come down.

Walking past me, Azhar asked me who the bowler was but I didn't know at that time. Dropped from the side a few months later, I came back as Mumbai captain and asked everybody who the bowler was: left-arm quick, big jump before delivery, a bit of a goatee. He was traced to National Club. I got him to bowl regularly in the nets. I didn't think the eighteen-year-old, Zaheer Khan from Shrirampur, was ready yet, but so proactive was the Mumbai system that they had him with the squad when we were travelling to Madhya Pradesh just because I had liked him and just so that he could gain from being around the Mumbai players. After I retired from first-class cricket, Baroda's Kiran More snapped Zaheer, but soon enough Tendulkar got him to come back to Mumbai.

So you can imagine the scene – scores of people just talking about upcoming talent in Mumbai. When they met each other, that's all they talked about. How a certain batsman was going to play for Mumbai in three years' time, what his strengths were and, yes, his weaknesses too. What he would need to do to excel at the highest level. They all were obsessed with the 'highest level'. If you succeeded at the highest level, only then did you fulfil your potential and made this community truly happy. They also prided themselves in knowing what was needed to succeed at the highest level even though they might not have made it to that level themselves.

In essence, this community was the marketing team of Mumbai's talent. Thanks to them, we in the 1986 Mumbai team were aware of Tendulkar and Kambli as two kids with prodigious talent, even though at that stage they were still playing school cricket. (They are doing the same with Prithvi Shaw at the moment.)

Years ago, I too had been marked out by this marketing team. They had watched me closely. I disappointed them because I was only getting attractive 30s and 40s. Dilip Sardesai was one of the high-profile members of this informal community. An international cricketer of great repute, Sardesai was happy to visit the maidans to watch local cricket with the sole purpose of finding a rough diamond in the dust of Mumbai city. Sardesai used to keep telling me and everyone else, including my father, that he did not have an issue with me getting five ducks in a row, but once I was set I couldn't afford to get out on 40. Because I kept doing exactly that, I noticed one season that Mumbai was starting to lose interest in me. All this changed on an inter-university tour to Baroda in 1985. That, though, is for later.

So when I look back, I remember myself as an average school cricketer. There were big stars in Giles Shield and Harris Shield who got hundreds in every second game. I could get just one per season. The selectors, though, were generally impressed with my batting style, especially my defensive technique – it was copybook. It was my natural technique; I don't remember cultivating it. It was my natural reaction when a ball was bowled to me.

To this marketing team of Mumbai cricket, big runs were not enough; they wanted tough runs. Runs against tough oppositions. So a hundred against an average team didn't impress them much. Perhaps they saw something in my technique and thought I could score those tough runs.

However, they didn't insist on one of the prerequisites of big and tough hundreds: fitness. All of us in that era grew up focusing only on skills and delivering in tough conditions. We were led to believe that physical fitness was not a necessary attribute to achieve this.

We were the complete opposites of arch-rivals Delhi, and cricketers from the north in general. They gave physical fitness great importance. Because Mumbai was winning more matches and had more players playing Tests and performing well against the best in the world, we felt mental toughness was all that was needed to be the best. Our seniors would point out to the sudden loss of fitness of north players when West Indies came calling. That's when Shastri would suddenly find himself batting in the top three even though he would bat at numbers 6 and 7 in home Tests. We grew up with near disdain for gym work and physical fitness.

That approach was a big mistake as I later found out in my career as India player, at the 'highest level'. If I had been fitter and stronger, I would not have been run out as much as I was in 1992. It's on tours like those in Australia that physical fitness of Indian players gets really tested. I also saw that on the 2011-12 tour as a commentator. At the end of an arduous tour where India lost all Tests and hardly won in the limited-overs format, the one man who stood strong right at the end of the tour was M.S. Dhoni. The rest looked sluggish when they were running between the wickets or chasing after a ball on those big outfields.

That devotion towards physical fitness didn't figure in the teachings of Mumbai batting and might have been one of the reasons why many Mumbai batsmen didn't reach the heights they could have. Tendulkar was naturally strong – like Gavaskar, even he had strong legs. This helped them along with their great skills to have long, successful careers.

*

During my time, Mumbai's cricketers had a systemic advantage over those from other states. If you had the talent and the hunger, everything around you was designed to take you to the highest level. You started off representing your school at the age of twelve or thirteen. The city schools are so obsessed with winning cricket tournaments that they even commit age fraud at times. Talented kids get all the possible encouragement and facilities if only out of the schools' vested interests in winning cricket tournaments.

If you happen to be at the right school, you sometimes get overqualified coaches too. Ramakant Achrekar, coach of Sharadashram Vidyamandir, used to take select wards to bat in four nets one after the other every day. The most celebrated of his wards was, of course, Tendulkar, who by the age of sixteen had batted as many hours as a regular twenty-year-old. Achrekar, a celebrated coach, had the power to get admissions for talented cricketers he spotted in the maidan. Chandrakant Pandit, former Indian keeper and a Mumbai stalwart, was an Achrekar discovery who got admission in Sharadashram.

Usually, it takes one man with the Achrekar-like passion to make a school team successful. At IES, my school in Dadar Hindu Colony, H.S. Bhor was that man. Although he was a PT teacher and wasn't qualified as a cricket coach, he wanted our school to have the best cricket team in Mumbai. I will never forget his joy when we won our maiden Giles Shield, the Under-15 inter-school tournament, in 1980. I was captain of that team. The final was all the more memorable for us not just because we won the prestigious tournament, but also because it was played at the Wankhede Stadium, a Test centre where all the greats played, and moreover a ground we had seen on television. This is how Mumbai encouraged school cricket, scheduling an inter-school final at a Test venue.

Our school's appointed cricket coach was Subhash Bandiwadekar, a seasoned Mumbai Ranji cricketer, a player too good to be coaching a school team. That's the quality of cricketers who would coach the little pockets of Mumbai city, grooming the next generation of cricketers. You had the guidance of seasoned cricketers in your teens, one of the most crucial phases for aspiring cricketers.

I remember once when I was fooling around towards the end of a nets session, bowling to bowlers – even they needed a hit sometimes. Bandiwadekar saw me roll a leg-break as a change-up delivery. He saw just one leg-break from me, and told me from then on I was to bowl more in the nets, and bowl only leg-spin. I began to do so regularly after my batting. I ended up making it to the India Under-19 camp as a leg-spinner. That's how good our school coaches were. Eventually I had to give up bowling to focus on my batting; I didn't like being an all-rounder. I wanted to be a pure top-order batsman, just like Sunil Gavaskar.

In many ways, Mumbai batsmen were privileged. We used to have a month-long camp of cricketers aged sixteen to nineteen at the Wankhede stadium. Teenage years are a delicate time in young cricketers' careers because that's when technique starts to set in.

At our camp, Dilip Sardesai oversaw us batsmen. That one month with him at the helm gave me brilliant new insights into batting, into what was needed to make it to the highest level. Only a player who has played at the international stage could have known the things he shared with us in that camp.

Sardesai opened our eyes to what batting discipline was truly about. In the nets, if a ball was bowled wide outside the off stump, out of habit we would just casually throw our bats at it. We were in the nets after all, and got only a certain number of deliveries to face, unlike at an actual match. This would drive Sardesai mad. 'What are you doing?' he would yell. 'Why do you want to give a chance to the bowler? If you want to play, play with conviction. Every ball, wherever it's bowled.' We were shocked by his reaction towards what we considered a non-event, but slowly realized that his approach was indeed batting discipline of the highest order.

Sandeep Patil as Mumbai captain reinforced the same kind of discipline when I played under him and batted with him in my first couple of years of Ranji cricket. During a long partnership, if he found that I was becoming a bit casual – and I didn't need to miss a ball, he could only look at me and convey from the non-striker's end: 'Sanjay, c'mon. You are looking a bit casual. C'mon. *Khadoos.*'

Patil came into my life at the right time. Between the age of eighteen and twenty-one, I had him right next to me on the field. Off it he would pick me up from home and drop me back after Ranji practice. While being driven to the Wankhede Stadium I would still be learning cricket stuff from him. If it wasn't cricket, I would be observing his effect on people. He was a big star then. If a senior international cricketer with leadership qualities plays Ranji cricket for a full season, it is invaluable to the youngsters in the Ranji team. Patil was that player for me. In my last two years as a cricketer, hopefully I was that cricketer to those who played under me in the Mumbai Ranji team.

During my younger days, Ravi Shastri and Dilip Vengsarkar, whenever they were free from national duty, would join us in the Mumbai team. Vengsarkar would even show up at the Times Cricket Shield matches. Like with Tendulkar, Vengsarkar was a huge supporter of me when I was coming up the ranks. Even if he was in the opposition, standing at first slip, whenever I would play a good shot, I could hear him say, 'Ah! Shot.' During drinks or a break, he would tell his friends, '*Kya chabuk batting karta hai.*' ['What crisp batting.'] Such comments can really boost one's confidence, especially if it's coming from someone like Vengsarkar. They are invaluable little doses of confidence that sort of make you believe that you are exceptional and on to greater things.

About Shastri, Chandrakant Pandit once told me how he saw him through to a hundred in a high profile Irani Cup match, by reminding himself – 'Don't cover-drive him' – every single time he faced Kapil. Shastri was one of the best senior cricketers I played with in the Indian team. Most of the cricketers in the Indian team I played in were guarded and insecure. Shastri, however, was an exception. He was rare because he took pride in others' performances. When I got my first Test hundred, against West Indies in Barbados, I came to know later that he had called V.S. Patil, who was his coach too at Mumbai's Podar college, congratulating him on giving India another '*dus saal ka ghoda*', a player who would serve India for ten years at least. Shastri soon became that senior player whom I went to for advice on all cricket-related matters.

Then there was Gavaskar. As I was getting close to my chances for my maiden call to the Indian team, I was due to play an India

Under-25 match against West Indies. At that time, the West Indies team was a frightening prospect – they had the pace, the skill and the endurance to keep hurting you all day long. There was a story around Michael Holding's bowling – they said that sometimes you couldn't even see the ball when he bowled at you. At the time, I used to work at Nirlon, and Gavaskar was a senior manager there with his own cabin. He would make sure he was in office when he was not playing or training. I sought an appointment with him.

'I want to know just one thing about West Indies; when you're facing them, do you actually not see the ball?' Gavaskar burst out laughing. Sitting in his chair, he then started demonstrating how to play them. He told me that they bowl into the body of any new batsman – quick, short, and into the body. If you got right behind it, he said, demonstrating that famous Sunil Gavaskar defence with the elbow right up while sitting in his chair, you should be fine. 'And, of course, you can see the ball!'

Mumbai players in that era had each other's back. It was something that I took for granted. It's only later, when I played for India, that I learnt that things could be different in a team game. I missed Mumbai at those times.

*

It would all begin just before the 6 a.m. alarm. The Bollywood term for it might be 'struggle' but for me it was fun – to grow up playing cricket in the city of Mumbai.

Being a team sport, you always had the company of like-minded boys on the same journey and with the same goals. You spoke the same secret language. '*Kaakdi*' in Marathi means cucumber, but for us cricketers that word was for everything that was brilliant.

'*Kaakdi* bat, *kaakdi* shot.' You laughed at the same jokes; you became a part of the Mumbai cricket humour. When two Mumbai cricketers meet after twenty years, it's this humour that binds them immediately, like instant glue.

As a schoolboy, I would sleep with the dream of taking part in this fun activity. My eyes used to open with eagerness just before the alarm went off. Then I would go to school where one could miss a few lessons to attend school practice in the afternoon. That made me feel special – I can't forget the expressions on the faces of the rest of the students as we swaggered out of the class and the school well before school actually got over.

Later, when I studied in Podar College, I would wake up before everybody, when it was still dark; I wanted to be the first to arrive at the Podar nets so that I'd get to bat first: After two or three batsmen had batted, the pitch would start to crumble away. The pitch was at its best if you batted first. We lost count of the number of batsmen who got hit batting late in those Podar nets.

Speaking of getting hit, I'm reminded of my friend Ashish Parulekar who today has a flawless set of front teeth. However, they are artificial: he lost the original set in the Podar nets at the age of seventeen. There were many like him who walked around wearing dentures at the age of twenty. That's why from an early age we had great respect for the hard cricket ball. We knew very early in our cricketing careers that the ball could really hurt us, if we weren't careful. Even when we started wearing helmets later in our careers, we felt protected all right, but the memories of what the ball could do weren't completely erased.

In fact, in those days, the hardness of the cricket ball was a big deal. Even at the senior level there were batsmen – good batsmen – who had a real fear of the ball, a fear of getting hit. These batsmen were easy to spot, and anyone not scared of the cricket ball was considered quite special. To get over the fear of the hard cricket ball was a basic challenge to conquer before we could move on to other issues of batting.

While the morning nets happened at Podar, the evening sessions took place in better facilities in south Mumbai, mostly at the Wankhede Stadium, in the Mumbai Under-15 and Under-19 nets. That was pretty much the schedule when we weren't playing matches: net practice every morning and evening. Just batting and bowling for hours; no strength conditioning. Even fielding practice was just once a week, which is why we hated Mondays.

We used to play a lot of matches though, and that used to be fun. Our Giles Shield matches would mostly be at the Cross Maidan in south Mumbai. We'd gather at school early in the morning to travel as a team together to 'town', which is what south Mumbai is still known as. Once everyone assembled, we'd carry our kits and walk from the school to the train station. 'Dagdu', the school peon whose formal name we didn't know, would carry the school kit – a huge sack containing kits for those who didn't have their own gear.

After a twenty-minute walk, we'd reach Dadar station and take the local train to Victoria Terminus (VT), now known as Chhatrapati Shivaji Terminus (CST). Being early in the morning, this was also the time when the whole of suburban Mumbai too would travel to VT, for work. We were quite a sight during this peak hours' rush – fifteen young schoolboy cricketers, lugging their big kit bags with them, Dagdu with his massive sack, and the coach, Bandiwadekar, and our PT teacher, Bhor, all trying to get in at one time into a packed compartment as the train stopped for only a few seconds.

Just like teams get into a huddle before stepping on to the field nowadays, we too would huddle to just go over the protocols once again: Let the passengers alighting get off first, don't stand in front of the exit, and once clear of the passengers getting off, charge into the compartment. Despite the maddening rush, it's amazing that we never left one from the group behind in over three years of train travels for inter-school matches.

We would be slightly tired by the time we reached VT, but the thought of our favourite breakfast would top up the excitement. It would always be the same restaurant: Aram, a short walk from VT station. The menu was fixed too: *missal*, a mix of savouries and hot curry, along with bread, jam and a cup of hot tea. The thought of this feast awaiting us would almost make us sprint from the station all the way to the restaurant. I wonder how parents would have reacted seeing us run like that, with cars and buses coming at us from all directions.

Food was a big deal for us during our matches. Islam Gymkhana, Cricket Club of India and Bombay Gymkhana were our favourite grounds because the lunch at all these places was great. During one of our school matches, Bhor sir felt he should treat us to some different food. He took us to New Empire Café, which served mutton cutlet for lunch with a little gravy and lots of bread. Our fielding standards dropped so dramatically after that meal that this was our last lunch at that café. We went back to our regular eating place: a south-Indian vegetarian restaurant.

It was a great time for us. Isolated from the real world and real-life problems, we just lived to fulfil our dreams. We all had one. Mine was to become famous. It was a great high seeing my name appear in newspapers. Fortunately, inter-school cricket got fairly good coverage in the newspapers back then. Headlines such as 'Sanjay Manjrekar Shines', 'Superb Knock by Sanjay' started appearing in the *Times of India*, *Indian Express* and *Free Press Journal*. This was the time I was slowly getting out of my father's shadow. I was now getting to be known as Sanjay Manjrekar, and not just as Vijay Manjrekar's son.

During my college days, I got my name screen-printed on my kit bag. Whenever I'd take the BEST bus to attend practice, I'd keep this bag close to me near my seat and make sure my name was visible in a way that my fellow passengers could read it properly. I'd discreetly watch their reactions when they read the name. Had they heard of me? Did a bell ring inside their heads when they read my name? I am quite embarrassed about all this now, but that was the driving force that got me to go through the yards, day in day out without a vacation, only to be well known.

I missed my eldest sister's wedding, because there was an important Under-19 match outside Mumbai on that day.

4

CALYPSO MAGIC

WHENEVER I TRAVELLED for cricket matches, I loved to come back with stories to thrill my friends with. While watching Imran Khan handle a mercurial Pakistan side in his own unique fashion, I would try to memorize the lines and the way Imran spoke to them even as I batted. Before my first international series away from home, though, I took one story with me.

West Indies were the undisputed kings of cricket then. When we reached the Caribbean islands in 1989, they had just come back after thrashing Australia 3–1 in Tests and dominating the triangular ODI series.

Once I knew I was going on the tour, I met with Sunil Gavaskar again, one of the few who had done well against their fast bowlers, for a chat about playing against West Indies. Among other things, I asked him if the West Indies bowlers sledge a lot. 'Nope,' he said. On the contrary, he said, they were just silent. In fact, I learnt that they were the quietest team to play against. They knew how good they were, and they didn't need to reinforce it verbally.

The only noise you heard was from the stands.

The end of an over, Gavaskar said, felt like the end of a day at school, where you'd see all the students pouring out from the building in a rush. As almost all the West Indies fielders used to be behind the stumps, you could hear them approach from behind you at the end of the over to take their positions at the other end. Indeed, throughout the tour, every time an over ended, I was reminded of kids running out of a school from behind me. Jeffrey Dujon, the five slip fielders, the gully – would all run past me, quietly.

The noisiest bunch, Gavaskar said, were the Pakistani players, but they too just had a go at each other, creating quite a racket. Pakistan sledged each other rather than the opposition. But West Indies were even more menacing because they didn't say anything. If at all anyone chirped, it was their slowest bowler Eldine Baptiste.

The same can't be said of the Caribbean people – they were a chirpy lot and loved a chat. We got a typical welcome on the streets. On our first day of nets in Barbados, when our bus stopped at the traffic lights, a man walked up to us and said, 'Oh, Indian players? Nice to have you here. Welcome to the West Indies. But sorry, we're going to beat you.' And he left. From my experience over the next two months, I know he truly meant both. He wanted to truly welcome us, but he was also confident they were going to beat us.

That man was not boasting. The West Indies fans knew their cricket, and loved it the right way. They loved the game, not the stars. They knew as much about the opposition as they did about their own team. They were particularly fond of the skilful Indian teams, especially the batsmen and the spinners. I was hardly a known face, but a man recognized me at a pharmacy once and began talking. Again, he welcomed me to the West Indies, and then fondly rattled out the names of all the players of the India team of 1971 that beat them 1–0. This was the famous side led by Ajit Wadekar, but this man recollected all the players' names, down to even stop-gap wicketkeeper Pochiah Krishnamurthy who never played a Test before or after that tour.

The name 'Krrrishna-mati' sounded so musical in Lord Realtor's 'Gavaskar' calypso. The early 1970s was a time when West Indies cricket was at a low but that never stopped them from appreciating the Indian team. Back then they 'couldn't out Gavaskar at all', but their fans knew things were different now.

Once these fans reached the stadium, they would become ruthless. They loved aggressive bowling. They loved bouncers. They loved that their tall fast bowlers tormented visiting batsmen. Every time somebody would bowl a bouncer there was excitement, an audible buzz around the stands. At the old Antigua Recreation Stadium, during an ODI, they had big speakers in the stands that played catchy local tunes. Arun Lal took a blow early in the match, and even as the Indian physio attended to him while he winced in pain, loud music blared from the speakers and the fans danced to it.

However, if a visiting player happened to provide them a contest, either blunting their fast bowlers or, especially, taking them on, they adored him. They weren't guys who just came to see West Indies win and went home unhappy if they lost. If somebody took them on, they loved that player. That's why they worshipped Gavaskar.

I was not quite Gavaskar but I felt their love after I scored a hundred in the Barbados Test. On the field, I found West Indies players to be the best opposition to play against. They knew they were a great side no matter what the conditions were. I could even sense some compassion towards the opposition because they realized how difficult it was for us to stand up to their bowling. I never saw that with any other opposition. You would have some of their senior players going out of their way to advise us and guide us. I suspect it was more out of wanting a good contest.

Since I had made my Test debut against them in Delhi and had played a couple of side games too, the West Indies players knew me when I went there. At functions when both teams would attend, Jeffrey Dujon started talking to me about my technique. He told me not to get on my toes to defend their short deliveries – he said I would lose my balance that way. He told me about the virtues of being grounded on the back foot even if the ball was a bouncer. Here was the world's best wicketkeeper, having taken the trouble of studying a rookie's technique and then sharing insights with him. That was priceless advice.

In my debut Test in Delhi, a bouncer from Winston Benjamin cut my eye and left me bleeding. Desmond Haynes was the first man to show concern for what had happened. I later saw pictures of me being taken off the field, and there Haynes was, next to me, holding my bat, pad and everything else as the Indian team doctor helped me off the field. Haynes walked me right till the edge of the boundary trying to make sure I was all right.

This gesture was nothing compared to what he did for me in the West Indies. Even today I still wonder if it indeed happened or if I'd been dreaming. We played the ODIs before the Tests and got hammered in every match. I didn't play any of these matches, but before every match Haynes would check with me during the warm-ups if I was playing that day. I would always say no, and he would shake his head in disappointment. And I would think – this guy is the opposition's opener and has his own worries, but he always checks on me.

Between the third and the fourth ODIs we played a first-class side game against West Indies Under-23 at St Kitts. A left-hand batsman scored a sensational 182 against us in that game. His drives had a power and sound that rang in your ears. This was our first introduction to a nineteen-year-old Brian Charles Lara. Before him, though, I too got a century. We went to Antigua for the next ODI, and during the warm-ups before the match there was Haynes, again with the same question to which I had the same answer.

'What? A hundred not good enough for your guys to pick you?' he asked in frustration. He would express similar views just before the fifth ODI.

The Guyana Test was to be my first international assignment on the tour, but I was told only minutes before the toss. I was taking a knock on the morning of the match not knowing whether I'd be playing or not, and I saw Haynes waving from the home dressing room. He was trying to catch my attention from the big window. When I looked towards him, he shouted, 'Well done, you are playing today.' He raised his thumb up for me and had a big smile on his face.

My eyes welled. Here was a West Indies great, concerned about me, whether I was going to get the break he thought I deserved. And when I got that chance finally, he had found it out before me and was happy for me. It would have been easy for him to focus only on his batting because he could be opening the innings in half an hour, but instead was worried enough about me that he found out from the Indian team whether I had been selected.

Years later, I got an opportunity to do some television work with Haynes for Ten Sports, and I told him exactly what I thought of him. He gave me that same endearing smile of his, the famous Desmond Haynes grin.

I am glad I didn't let Haynes down, and scored a hundred in my second Test there, in Barbados. We lost the Test, and on the last day as I walked towards the team bus, a familiar figure was waiting in the parking lot. It was the king himself, Viv Richards, and he was waiting for … me. Mind you, Richards was not a friendly guy on the field. Haynes would spend a lot of time in the Indian dressing room, but Richards perhaps consciously stayed unfriendly not to lose that competitive edge he was so proud of.

Richards called me out and said, 'Can I have a word with you?' I went up to him and that ruthless competitor on the field shook my hand warmly and said, 'Well played, man. Keep it up.'

We had grown up watching these superstars on rented VHS tapes. My friend Sanjay Pednekar used to arrange the TV, the bulky cassette player and the tapes and used to watch the highlights of Channel 9's coverage of the World Series Cricket and other Australia–West Indies series for hours. When the titles started rolling I would feel a tingle of nervous excitement.

Wherever West Indies went they arrived like gods. They were all big and imposing; they had the confidence of knowing they were the best; they were chirpy wherever they went. It was an arresting sight. They walked around like they owned the place, and Richards was always in the forefront and in the spotlight. Now he had actually taken the trouble of waiting there for me, just to congratulate me.

Right towards the end of the tour, during the final Test, in Jamaica, I was walking up the corridor of my hotel floor to get to my room when I saw Malcolm Marshall running towards me. I stopped in my tracks and played a shadow defensive shot and said, 'Shit, I thought you were coming to bowl at me again.'

Marshall was actually in a hurry and wanted to rush to the lift. He still stopped briefly and said, 'Oh, don't worry. No bowling now, but you know what, I want to talk to you after the series gets over. Not now because we still have a few days of cricket left.' And he winked and left.

Sure enough, after the series was over, after we had lost another Test, I got word in the dressing room that Mr Marshall was waiting for me outside. He had actually waited for five minutes before sending the message in. Arguably the best fast bowler of all time, waiting outside the opposition dressing room, for what? For talking cricket with a twenty-three-year-old rookie. And he only had good advice, on how to adjust to English pitches, for example, after the hard, bouncy ones of the West Indies.

I think I had earned his respect through our on-field back-and-forths. In the Barbados Test, during my century, I had played Marshall comfortably. It was Curtly Ambrose and Ian Bishop who troubled me. Come the next Test in Trinidad, and the great mind of Marshall had worked me out. He got me out cheaply in both innings with balls coming back into me.

Manjrekar lbw Marshall 0 in first innings.

Manjrekar lbw Marshall 1 in the second.

Coming in to Jamaica, I did a bit of homework of my own. When I came up to bat, Marshall began with a few short balls and then a few outswingers. I knew he was setting me up for the inswinger. When that inswinger arrived, my pad didn't go too far across and my bat came nice and straight to play the ball back where it came from. Marshall didn't say anything in his follow-through, but I could see in his stare that he acknowledged the fact that I had seen what he was up to and had corrected my weakness. That an opponent was not a sitting duck and made him work hard made Marshall happy.

So there I was, in the West Indies amidst the incredible cricketers I had watched on TV, and interacted with them and was liked by them. All these experiences were dizzying for a twenty-three-year-old. I could see that for them it was not just about winning, it was also about making the game greater. First, by themselves becoming role models and then helping talent from all over the world achieve their potential. They were there to make the cricketing world a better place.

If they played cricket in the right spirit, the West Indies cricketers and fans expected nothing less in return. Marshall never forgave Dilip Vengsarkar for some gamesmanship that the latter had indulged in – this was way before I debuted for India, but on that tour I got a first-hand experience of the righteous way they expected their opponents to play.

Coming into Jamaica, Richards surprisingly had scored only twenty-five runs in three Tests even as others plundered us. In the final Test, though, he struck form and scored a masterful century. But the great champion that Richards was, he was not satisfied with just a hundred; we could see he was determined to make this a big one.

We heard two sounds. In domestic cricket, we used to appeal not only when we thought the batsman was out but also when we thought the umpire was likely to raise his finger. When we heard those two sounds, our cheeky wicketkeeper Kiran More went up in appeal. So did the rest of us, even though we knew there was no bat involved. Some people call it cheating, some gamesmanship, but we were about to learn it was simply not acceptable when playing in the West Indies.

The umpire raised the finger, and Richards could not believe it. His reaction was like a child's. He was not upset that the umpire had made a mistake; he just couldn't believe someone had indeed appealed when there had been no bat involved. His problem was More, not the umpire David Archer. He stood his ground for a while, stomped the surface and then dragged himself off, all the while glaring at More. It was quite clear to us that Richards felt More had cheated him.

My first reaction was to think what a great batsman he was, that he wanted to make up for a poor series with a big hundred, that he was reacting like he had been given out on 20 and not 110. The crowd, however, thought otherwise. Their king had been seen off, and his anger was apparent. So they protested. They began to throw onto the field whatever they could get their hands on. Chants of 'More is a teef' ['More is a thief'] rang around the stadium.

It looked like the Test would end prematurely when even the police couldn't control the chaos. Local heroes Dujon and Courtney Walsh came out to pacify the crowd but failed. In the end, it was Richards himself who had to come out of the dressing room and appeal for peace. Signs of his disappointment were still visible in how he still had his thigh pad and the whites on when he walked out towards the stands. 'It's okay,' he said, appealing towards them to calm down. 'I'm okay, please relax and let's get this game on the way.' The Test resumed, and we went on to duly lose it.

It was a good thing this was the last Test of the series because More was haunted by the words 'More is a teef' wherever he went till the end of the series. In those days, security arrangements at cricketing venues were fairly relaxed and quite a few irate fans had access to the Indian keeper. I don't know though if More ever found the courage to walk up to Richards and straighten things out.

*

The one thing that I brought back from the West Indies, the one thing I couldn't wait to tell my friends about on my return was their slip catching. People didn't talk about their slip cordon as much as their bowling, but coming from India, where slip-catching wasn't great, I could feel the difference. It was just my luck that my first few Tests were against West Indies. If you edged a ball that went past your bat, there was no need to look behind. There was like a net behind you. If you edged, you just walked.

We were brought up playing with the Khanna Winsrex ball in domestic cricket. It was basically a smooth round stone with some lacquer on it and it just flew off the edges. Some slippers caught it, but most just pretended to go for catches. Those Winsrex balls broke many fingers at the first-class level. Thankfully, it was not used in international matches. However, in one festival game in 1987 they got us to play with it. One of the West Indies pacemen saw the ball and said, 'I could kill someone with this.'

When we went to South Africa in 1993, I was again awed by the slip catching of Brian McMillan. I remember he once had a batsman dropped twice off his bowling, and in the next over he effortlessly snaffled a low chance with his bucket palms and banged the ball into the ground as if to ask, 'Who will take catches off my bowling?' Those two chances, incidentally, were the only ones their team dropped in the entire tour.

The West Indies slip cordon, though, was something else. It

was intimidating to look back at them because they would stand almost three-fourths of the way to the boundary. As you waited in the dressing room, awaiting your turn, you'd watch all that was happening outside – a nerve-racking wait. And then when a wicket fell and you went out, you realized it was completely different out there. You took your guard, saw the bowler at the top of his mark, and realized that now it's just him and you. If you happened to look back at Dujon and the slip cordon, it hit you that they were expecting the ball to carry all the way back. It had the same impact as looking at an angry Patrick Patterson at the top of his mark.

The first time I was in the middle, I was intimidated, but then I had stopped looking. I would note how many slips and gullies they had, but made a conscious effort not to make a note of the distance.

I did make a note, though, of what a fun side they were to watch. They just had fun on the field. Their skill and their fitness was far superior. Despite being from different island nations, despite all the politics, they took much more pride in their performance.

On India's 2016 tour of the West Indies, I got a chance to work in close proximity with Viv Richards. We were both commentating on a lop-sided Indian win, but I got an insight into what made Richards the great competitor that he was. Of course, he had exceptional batting skills, but his pride drove him to do that bit extra. He believed he was second to none. And that is why when he played cricket, he wanted his team to be second to none.

Even now, Richards came to the ground every day hoping that this current West Indies team would show the same qualities that his team did. As West Indies went from one defeat to another, his heart never sank. He would come to work with renewed vigour every day, hoping that today things would change. Even as an expert, when I would ask him if he thought West Indies could last three sessions against the India bowlers, he never said no, even though we all knew the answer.

Richards kept saying, 'They can, if they believe in themselves and play with pride.' Because that's what he did, and that's what his team had always done. Our studio shows for the matches were on the ground by the boundary. In the commercial breaks, he would keep shouting out at some player or the other, pumping his fist in the air, 'C'mon, you can do it.'

The great West Indies team had all the natural attributes but what made them winners was the fierce pride they had as individuals. In the Guyana Test of 1989, there was only two days' play possible because of rain. One evening Ravi Shastri and I were sitting in the balcony, having a quiet cup of tea, when we heard the ball repeatedly thudding into the net. We saw two Antiguans, Curtly Ambrose and Richie Richardson, both at their peak. There was some needling going on between the two. And this is no exaggeration: Richardson couldn't lay bat on ball. Ambrose kept running in. Every ball would be short of length, would square Richardson up, pass him by his chest and upwards and thud into the net so hard that the whole net area shook. Richardson was lucky he didn't get hurt.

Shastri and I looked at each other. We didn't need to say anything. We knew what a tough test awaited us. Both of us went on to get hundreds in the next Test. Two Podar college boys, two V.S. Patil wards, had conquered their fears once again. Just like they did as eighteen-year-olds in the dodgy Podar nets almost every morning at 7 a.m.

But this time we did it without the guidance of a dedicated coach such as Patil, and without any preparation as a team. Our preparation to take on the giants of world cricket was practically zero. We did our preparations individually. We faced tennis balls dipped in water chucked at us short and fast on a concrete surface. Shastri told me how he stood outside the crease in his stance so that he could meet the short ball before it reached its highest bounce. When I innocently asked him what if the bowler dug it in shorter, he didn't have an answer. It was 'whatever works'.

We didn't have a specialized coach, unlike the multitude today – batting coach, bowling coach, fielding coach. We had just a manager who doubled up as coach to give us the odd cricket advice and help the captain pick the team. Our man on that tour was fond of his afternoon naps. When I got the hundred in the side game at St Kitts – the innings that failed to get me selected for the remaining ODIs – I came back to see our manager fast asleep in the dressing room. Later, on another tour, Dilip Vengsarkar sang the song '*Jaago Mohan Pyare*' to wake up another team coach who was found dozing off on the floor of the dressing room when we returned from the field.

It was up to the player as to how much he wanted to contribute to the team, how much he wanted to get involved. This West Indies tour was like all other overseas tours: There was no question of winning. Success for the Indian team was the one hundred or two hundreds in the series or a five-wicket haul. Winning was left for later when a home series came along.

5
PAKISTAN

MY FIRST DAY of international cricket in Pakistan is one I will never forget. It was the afternoon session in Karachi, Pakistan were batting and I was fielding at mid-on. Suddenly from behind me I heard someone muttering something about 'Kashmir' and 'you Indians'. I looked back to see a person in a grey Pathani suit walk past me and head towards the pitch. He had just nonchalantly walked in with a Test match going on. When he reached the pitch, he started shouting anti-India slogans – basically, telling us we shouldn't have come on tour. As the fielding team, we didn't know what to do, so most of us just stayed in our places hoping that the people who were supposed to take care of such matters would do their job.

The umpires tried to intervene, but the man went straight for the then Indian captain, Kris Srikkanth. The next thing we saw, to our utter shock and disbelief, was Srikkanth and the man exchanging blows. I couldn't believe what I was seeing. Srikkanth was now holding him by his shirt, and there was pulling and tugging from both sides. It was a street fight, except that it was happening during a Test match, and one of the persons involved was the India Test captain.

Within seconds, a few other players joined the fight. The man was surrounded by the Indian players. I don't clearly recall who all were there but Kiran More, always the team man, definitely got involved. I found it a little funny, watching More, with his pads on, trying to kick the intruder through all the legs and bodies that had surrounded him. It was also slightly amusing that the only fallout of this was Srikkanth going off the field for a couple of overs to change his shirt after he had lost all the buttons in the scuffle. The Test match continued as if nothing had happened. If this had happened today, the series would have been called off.

We now know that such an incident is no laughing matter, but this was 1989 and those were different days. Pakistan was a different country. They were also a different cricket team, unlike any other team the world had seen. We got a sample of that even before the first Test started.

Both the teams were practising in the evening session when we suddenly saw the legendary leg-spinner Abdul Qadir sprinting after a man. At first we wondered if that man was with the team, but he was a random spectator, one of the hundreds who had assembled at the National Stadium to watch us train. They had wandered onto the field as our practice went on. And there was Qadir, running after him as if his life depended on it. The rest of the crowd started to watch it and enjoy it. This man was younger and fitter than Qadir, and just as Qadir would get close to him, he would suddenly change direction. The chase went on for about five minutes. Both the teams stopped doing whatever they were doing, and began to watch this spectacle: a great leg-spinner running after a fan during a practice session before a Test match.

Eventually the chase came to an end when the security joined in. Maybe Qadir was allowed to have a couple of swipes at the man before they let him go. The show was over, and we went back to our practice sessions. There was nothing in the papers the next morning either. We were later told by a Pakistan player – in a hush-hush manner – that the man had pinched Qadir's bottom during the practice session.

Pakistanis were known to be emotional cricketers. At times, they resembled a dysfunctional family, constantly quarrelling but coming together when it mattered. Undoubtedly, they had exceptional talent, but they needed a patriarch to bring them all together. That patriarch was my biggest take-away from that tour. When I came back from that tour, I was dying to tell my friends about the man who had now matched, perhaps surpassed, Sunil Gavaskar as my cricket idol.

I could find no fault with Imran Khan Niazi. He had me even before hello. Those were the days when the Pakistan team was notorious for fielding thirteen men against the opposition – Shakoor Rana and Khizer Hayat or any of their two local umpires providing them great support. Call them patriotic if you wish, all their success at home had an asterisk attached to it. But Imran said, 'No more.' And in that big series against arch rivals India, he single-handedly ensured we had neutral umpires, John Hampshire and John Holder, both from England.

It became clear that Imran had the will – and the necessary influence – to make such far-reaching changes to improve the perception of his team. He wanted the world to see his team beat India without help from the umpires. He was willing to risk losing in this endeavour, but as we found out over the next four Tests, it was not easy to beat a side led by such a fierce competitor.

Imran was thirty-seven years old at the time. He had lost all his pace by then, but we never felt we could target him in the field or when he was bowling or when he batted. It was absolutely incredible watching him throughout that series. I don't recall a single moment on the field on that trip when Imran's attention drifted away from what was happening in the centre. We could be piling on the runs, it could be a long hot day in the field, but there was not one moment where you could see him looking in the direction of the stands or seeming bored. His eyes were always focused on what was happening on the field.

Things obviously didn't go as per plan for Pakistan as we managed to draw all the four Tests of that series. Barring the last Test in Sialkot, we got flat pitches everywhere. They started off being green but went back to their natural state as the match went on. There were a lot of overs to be bowled on long, hard days. Wasim Akram and Waqar Younis were the new pace sensations, but Imran knew they needed to be used sparingly as strike weapons; they had to be preserved as out-and-out quicks should be. Waqar had some fitness issues, so he played only two Tests. Imran, though, kept running in ball after ball on those flat pitches with the old ball, and sent down 185.3 overs in that series. On either side, only Wasim bowled more than Imran.

It was not just the number of overs he bowled, it was his intensity that stood out. Imran was a metronome as a bowler. Primarily, he was a major in-swing bowler so his aim used to be to start wide outside off and end up on the off stump. He did that for almost every ball for the 25–30 overs he bowled every day.

On the odd occasion that the ball finished on the middle stump and I was able to flick it for runs on the leg side, he would get absolutely livid with himself. I would then get to hear him utter the choicest of abuses in Punjabi and English. Even if it was just one run to square leg, the fact that he had allowed the batsman to play on the leg side was a big failure in his opinion. He was merciless on himself, and he expected the same from others.

In Lahore, when I was taking a single to bring up my double-century, I could hear Imran berating the bowler for allowing me to get an easy one on the leg side. I don't remember whether he applauded when I reached the landmark. Later in the series when Shoaib Mohammad was about to reach his landmark we had Srikkanth and More bowling.

I remember there was a match where we got confused if it was an one-day international or an exhibition game. With no agreement forthcoming, one team started out playing thinking it was a serious match, and the other team played it like an exhibition match. With Imran in one of the teams, you didn't need to guess which side took the game seriously. So we had Srikkanth clowning around with the ball, doing impressions of Qadir's action, and Imran watching it all with a deadpan expression. After bowling a long hop at Imran, Srikkanth smiled, but Imran just stared back with a straight face.

In the Faisalabad Test, Sachin Tendulkar got a light feather of a touch on the ball as he looked to work it off his hip. It was such a faint edge that no one appealed. Except Imran Khan, who was at mid-on. The umpire shook his head, but Imran was convinced there was some bat in that one. He kept asking his players how come they didn't hear it. '*Awaaz to zaroor aayi yaar* [There was definitely a sound],' he kept saying before he reluctantly dragged his feet back to mid-on.

At the end of the over, Tendulkar and I got together and he said, 'What a guy. What sharp ears.' He knew he had edged it. The wicketkeeper didn't hear it, the umpire didn't hear it, but the man at mid-on did. No one was as focused on the game as Imran was.

The cricket field was a place where Imran would let himself go. Captaining a team known for rustic behaviour, he would become the biggest rascal of them all. His cursing was a big part of his cricket. We knew he studied at Oxford and spoke charmingly, but it was a sight to behold when he let it rip at himself or his team-mates in the language of the common Pakistani man. Wasim and Waqar imitate Imran brilliantly. Whenever Wasim does it, a generous dose of swear words is a big part of the script. Imran truly felt at home on a cricket field, and expressed himself without a filter.

That he could connect with everyone in his team was a reason why he led Pakistan so successfully. They were a difficult side to lead. A side whose superstar batsman Javed Miandad enjoyed so much influence that he could ask for and get a flat pitch in Lahore for his hundredth Test despite his captain's wish to play on surfaces that help his young sensational quicks.

Because of the flat pitches, a typical Test for Imran would mean bowling 35–40 overs in an innings as we scored 400 or upwards. In the ten-minute break between innings, Imran – a lower-middle-order batsman – would come out all padded up to have a knock. He would repeat it in every break – lunch, tea – while his team batted. He would always have his full gear on as he came out for the knock.

On occasion if my eye wandered towards the dressing rooms when Pakistan were batting, I could see Imran fooling around with either the bat or the ball as he sat in the balcony. We had one such player in our dressing room too, but he was sixteen years old and on his first international tour. Imran, meanwhile was thirty-seven, and had been an international cricketer for eighteen years by then.

Imran's methods as captain made so much sense. It may have looked crude at times but it was effective especially given Pakistan's temperament. He could sense when a batsman was losing concentration; he would send out messages through substitutes. He could see an event before it happened and avert disasters.

There was no one in the Indian team to do such things. To be fair, Sandeep Patil did that to us, but only at the Ranji level. As a commentator, I once suggested M.S. Dhoni to become more hands on, to get into the head of someone like Umesh Yadav, to use a combination of Yadav's skill and fitness and Dhoni's brain. For this is what I had seen Imran do from mid-on with Wasim and Waqar.

There are great stories of how Imran used to mentor the young fast bowlers. When Pakistan went to England in 1990, Waqar was at his prime. Once, Allan Lamb on-drove him past mid-on, past Imran. Imran didn't exactly fancy chasing the ball, which pulled up inches outside the boundary. Imran came all the way back with the ball in his hand and asked Waqar, 'Vicky, what did you do there?'

Waqar replied, 'Skipper, I tried to bowl an inswinger to him.'

Imran threw up his arms in the air, and cried out to Waqar, 'Yaar, ask me before you do any such thing.'

A young bowler once stood at the top of his run and didn't run in right away. After a few seconds passed, Imran shouted at him from mid-on, 'Why aren't you bowling?' The reply was: 'You didn't tell me what to bowl.'

Both Tendulkar and I were so inspired by Imran's and then the South African way of bowling – machine-like outside the off stump and waiting for the batsmen to make mistakes – that we copied those styles when we played for Mumbai. We had an incredible time doing that. We destroyed all our opposition this way. All Mumbai bowlers bowled every ball as per our directives. They were the better for it. It was only when Ajit Agarkar came along in my last year as Mumbai captain that I felt I didn't need to tell him anything.

As with the great West Indies players, Imran wanted to play the game the right way. In 1992, we played Pakistan in a series of three matches in England to raise funds for Imran's hospital. The first was played at Crystal Palace in London. Even though they were exhibition matches, the fervour among fans did not diminish. If anything, they got a freer hand than at international matches. There were pitch invasions and missiles. The 42-over contest was reduced to 40, and eventually 25. Pakistan needed 69 runs in 7.5 overs when their fans made another invasion, forcing the organizers to abandon the game. At the post-match presentations, Imran grabbed the microphone and announced that India had won this game and said the Pakistan fans' behaviour was shameful.

In my first personal encounter with Imran, I was afraid I had infuriated my hero similarly. This was from a Sharjah tour before we went to Pakistan in 1989. We were at the ground for an India–Pakistan match. I was taking a knock before the match when I hit a ball that went in the direction of some Pakistani journalists standing just outside the boundary. It nearly cleaned out one of them as they all ducked for cover. One of them shouted at me, 'Play these shots in the match, not here.'

I was a young hothead then, and saw this remark as one coming from someone who was part of the dominant camp in Sharjah. Pakistan were a superb side respected all over the world, and when it came to Sharjah they were the kings. Teams just turned up in Sharjah to take their beating from Pakistan. The Indian team went there twice a year, so I guess we bore the brunt more than the others. That's why I thought that the offended journalist was being arrogant.

That made me angry, and I told him he should be in the press box and not in the ground. The journalist was in no mood to step back, and we had a spat. Raman Lamba had to intervene and drag me away. The matter didn't end there, though. At the Sharjah Cricket Stadium you have to walk through a common lounge area to get to your respective dressing rooms. As I walked back through there, one of my team-mates asked me what had happened, and I said, 'Nothing, just some Pakistani rascal trying to act smart.'

Then I felt a tap on my shoulder, and that unmistakable loud booming voice told me, 'Don't be so anti-Pakistani.'

Months later, when I was in awe of Imran during that Pakistan tour, I was always reminded of how I had begun on the wrong foot with my hero. I wondered if Imran held that against me still. I wondered if that was the reason he swore at his bowler for letting me take the 200th run easily in Lahore. I wondered if I could ever be on friendly terms with Imran.

*

The 1989 tour came and went. Imran didn't speak a word to me on the field through the four Tests. Once the series was over, though, Imran was lavish in his praise for me on every public platform. I realized now that to Imran the Sharjah incident might have been so trivial he possibly didn't even remember it. As with all great ambassadors of the game, it was good cricket that mattered to him. To get such admiration from my idol was the biggest prize for my performance in Pakistan.

Our next interaction came after I had a lukewarm tour of New Zealand. The moment he saw me he asked me, 'Why did you play Richard Hadlee off the back foot?' He told me I played Wasim and Waqar well because I was looking to move forward all the time. While it was sound technical advice, I was just floored that my hero liked my batting enough to follow that tour and be disappointed with my failures. This was a Pakistani following the progress of an Indian and wanting him to do well.

I was not the only one. This was the time Maninder Singh had developed his yips and had lost his run-up, his action, his zip. A prodigious talent with a beautiful action, Maninder was a shadow of himself now. After speaking to me, Imran headed straight to Maninder and asked him, 'Manni, what have you done to your bowling? Why did you change your action? There is no run-up now, nothing.'

Maninder tried to reason with him by saying he had lost his accuracy and had to shorten his run-up to regain the control, but Imran was having none of it. 'If I lose my accuracy I can't shorten my run-up,' Imran said. 'I will lose all my pace. This is not done. Go back to the original run-up and keep bowling at one stump, a thousand balls a day, and you will find your accuracy.'

Imran was not born to be a great. He had to work hard and put himself through tremendous grind to achieve greatness. Plus, he was a generous man to boot. These are the people who have a lot of cricket wisdom to share and pass on rather than the ridiculously talented cricketers.

Ramiz Raja once told me that if Imran had been my captain he would have never dropped me and would have ensured that I succeeded at all cost. He was that kind of a leader. If he believed in someone, he backed that player fully. Inzamam-ul-Haq was a beneficiary of Imran's trust. Even before Imran took him to the World Cup in Australia and New Zealand, Imran had announced to the world that they had found the next great batsman. When Inzamam failed at No. 3 in the 1992 World Cup, the thirty-nine-year-old Imran pushed himself up to No. 3 but never dropped Inzamam, who eventually won them the semi-final against New Zealand.

Imran and the other seniors around him had incredible self-belief. They thought their team was second to none, no matter where they played or against whom they played. There weren't too many around in India to do what Imran did for Inzamam.

Imran also knew his players inside out. Ramiz told me how he would settle differences within the team. There was this one time when Saleem Yousuf and Javed Miandad got into a bit of a fight on the field. They were both strong characters, and neither man was willing to take a step back. During the lunch break, an upset Miandad went up to Imran and said that either Yousuf was going to stay on the tour or he was; that the team was too small for both Yousuf and him.

Imran listened to him and said, '*Yaar Javed tu bhi na...* [Javed, you are impossible]' Imran then laughed and left. That was it. That was the end of the fight. It was incredible. With any other captain, who knows how much this issue would have escalated. Imran, though, knew Javed well enough to handle him the way he did, and he also had the stature and the intelligence to trivialize this threat.

Ramiz has often told me he never ever heard one negative thought expressed in the Pakistan dressing room during Imran's tenure as captain. He still wonders where Imran got the confidence from to say they were going to win the World Cup the moment they landed in Australia in 1992. Even when Pakistan played West

Indies, they would go in with positivity. Not one defensive word was said. He spread this positivity all around.

It will forever be my regret that we had no Imran-like senior in our dressing room. Youngsters like Kiran More and Manoj Prabhakar would have gained a lot under Imran; they were the kind of players Imran backed. Ijaz Ahmed once batted conservatively at the end of an ODI innings, and came back with a score 30-odd not out. Imran told him he would be sent back home if he put his personal interests ahead of the team ever again. In India, meanwhile, More found himself batting higher in the order against formidable attacks because more accomplished senior players chose to take the easy way out by dropping themselves down the order.

Similarly, Prabhakar ended up opening with the bat in 23 of his 39 Tests. These two were also a little Pakistani when it came to temperament. Contrary to the narrative of a bitter rivalry between the India and Pakistan teams, we got along pretty well. The rivalry was more among the fans, who were in each other's faces, and the media. In Pakistan in 1989 for over two months, there was not a single instance of any fight or a face-off between the players – except that Prabhakar and More always tried getting under the skin of Miandad, who was not one to take it lying down. The unforgettable More–Miandad incident that we saw in the 1992 World Cup was at least three years in the making.

In Australia, Imran wanted to beat us on green pitches because he had the resources, but when we reached Lahore we saw a flat track. We found it strange but then someone made the connection that this was Miandad's 100th Test, and he had had a word with the match curator. It was, of course, his greatness that he said he wanted to get a hundred in his 100th Test, and even on a flat deck it can't be easy to say it and deliver it, which he duly did.

When Miandad came out to bat, he had a song on his lips. It was obvious he was singing to get rid of the nerves, but More didn't let him forget it. A bizarre conversation followed, as Miandad took guard: More asked him which song he was singing as he walked out, and he told him the details of the song.

While More would irritate Miandad with his antics, Prabhakar used to tell Miandad he will make him disco-dance with his swing. Prabhakar was the first bowler in our team to learn reverse swing. He showed how to do it to Kapil Dev, who was more of a purist. It was the mischievous brain of Prabhakar that learnt this art.

I played for two months in Pakistan and did quite well against some of the best practitioners of reverse swing, but I had no idea what exactly the phenomenon was. I had no idea where the shiny side and the rough side was. I just watched the ball till as late as possible and reacted accordingly.

Someone told me later about the shiny side and the rough side and how you could get an idea beforehand if you watched the sides carefully. I remember sharing this with Mohammad Azharuddin, sometime in the mid-nineties. He too had no clue about this trick until then. This proves one important thing about batting: If you watch the ball close and play late you can handle anything without complicating it too much.

It's not as if Pakistan were the most cohesive unit of all time, but at least it was more fun than malice. Their turning on each other in full public view – and they did so endearingly – made them a fun side to watch. It was loud when you went out to bat against Pakistan, but the noise would be their fielders sledging each other. They would quarrel with each other on the field. They were constantly at each other when Imran wasn't near.

There were no glares or shrugs of shoulders at misfields, only the choicest abuse, especially from Imran. I would be memorizing the great one-liners to repeat them to my friends once I got back – I'd imagine how thrilled they would be when I told them of how Imran behaved on the field.

Miandad would constantly be in Imran's ear with this advice or the other. Imran would at best tolerate him. I never saw Imran listen to advice from Miandad – a great in his own right – seriously. I never saw Miandad let up either. Then when it would get too much, you would hear Imran's booming voice: '*Yaar Javed tu rehne de. Ek baar kuch bolta hai phir doosri baar kuch aur bolta hai* [You let it be, Javed. You give one advice one moment, and something completely different the next moment].' Miandad would go back to the slip cordon muttering under his breath that things would be better if done his way.

Somebody once asked Imran if Miandad's advice ever worked for him and Pakistan at an important stage in any match. Imran's reply was that if somebody gave you a thousand suggestions a day, one or two were bound to work.

At times, it would get comical, but Pakistan knew how to win matches. That's where India and Pakistan were different at that time. We just carried with us a lot of self-doubt and negativity when we left our shores. While we would easily lose to England in England, Pakistan would go there and hammer them. In 1990, after we were done in England, Pakistan came and not only thrashed England but also beat all counties outright in the side games only because there was financial jackpot to be won if any team did that.

Even when we went to Sharjah, known for its flat pitches, it seemed we were there just to accept our punishment. Indeed, Sharjah was where the India–Pakistan rivalry would grow in intensity, perhaps thanks to the Pakistani fans in Sharjah. From the moment we landed at the airport, they would be in our faces. At the hotel, at the restaurants, at the shopping centres, and in the ground where the stands were so close to the playing area it seemed they could stretch their arms and touch us. Chants of '*Jivey, jivey*, Pakistan [Long live Pakistan]' haunted us everywhere.

Other than that, especially now that I look back, playing Pakistan was not as tough as people think. All the drama and the tension, the history between the two nations, the emotion that came with the matches, were external. As players, we weren't nearly as intense or edgy about facing off against each other as the fans were. In fact, we played against each other so many times that it eased our equation a bit.

Playing Pakistan was a far easier challenge than playing England, South Africa or Australia in their backyards. For starters, you played them mostly in Asia, many times in Sharjah – the flattest pitches you could get. I don't rate batting performances in Sharjah very highly. I once got the Man of the Series award there. It's not something I wear as a badge of honour.

There used to be a graveyard near the Sharjah Stadium. Every time we travelled to the ground, I used to wonder if the signage pointing towards the graveyard should actually point towards the ground; it was after all a graveyard for bowlers. 'Sharjah Stadium, where great bowlers' spirits come to die.' I once lofted Curtly Ambrose straight over his head in Sharjah. His next ball to me was a slower ball on my pads. It was like a tiger had been reduced to eating grass. That's what Sharjah did to bowlers, barring, of course, the Pakistani bowlers.

Other than losing to Pakistan as often as we and other teams did, there was much to like about playing in Sharjah. It was a good concept. Cricket boards got wealthier; former cricketers got the support they needed through the Cricketers' Benefit Fund Series (CBFS); and while active players didn't hit the jackpot quite like they have done with the Indian Premier League (IPL), it was still a heftier pay cheque than other formats of cricket.

The fans loved it too. The Indian fans would often have only two things to say. 'When are you playing next in Sharjah?' Upon getting an answer they would go: 'Please beat Pakistan the next time.' The odd electronics item as a gift was not considered out of place. One of Tendulkar's fans once gave him a Walkman. He and that yellow Walkman were inseparable for years. Life was simple – free gifts were a thrill for us.

The organizers at Sharjah had everything sorted. It was just a drilled routine for everyone involved. When we would land at the Dubai airport as a team, Asif Iqbal, former Pakistan cricketer and an organizer now, would be there to receive us. There would be a few hundred outside the airport, mostly shouting pro-Pakistan slogans, with a few Indians straying to measure up.

We would be put in a minibus with a trolley attached to the bus to carry our suitcases and kitbags. A short drive and we would arrive at the same hotel where the CBFS hospitality team would receive us and make sure we didn't feel any inconvenience. When we would reach the ground, our practice pitches would be ready with mineral water bottles laid out. It was all very professionally run, but in the light of the match-fixing allegations that emerged later and clouded Sharjah's reputation as a cricketing venue, one does tend to look back at things differently.

The India–Pakistan match on 23 October 1991 falls in this category. There had been overnight rain, which meant we were not able to start on time. At the time, there were no floodlights, yet we were told it was to be a 50-over game, which gives me hope that the farce that followed was just unprofessional than something dubious.

We were chasing 258. Tendulkar and I were going well in a partnership that eventually ended at 85 runs. Around the 42nd over of the chase, the light became unplayable. It was October and this was natural. We really should have played a shortened game, but worse was to follow.

Now there were no set playing conditions on how the winner was to be determined if a match were to be stopped prematurely. The Duckworth-Lewis system had not arrived yet. There could have been two possible methods to decide who would be the winner if we were to come off the field for bad light. On the comparative-scores method, we were ahead of Pakistan at the end of the 42nd over, but if the run-rate rule had to be applied, things could become complicated.

The run-rate rule was complicated enough in itself. For example, if we were to come off at the end of the 45th over, which is when we were eventually offered light, in order to win we had to be ahead of not just their score at the end of the 45th over but also what they had scored in their last five overs. However, because we had conceded plenty in our last five overs – thanks to Imran who scored 43 off just 24 balls – we were sure to lose on the run-rate method.

Out in the middle, as evening set in and street lights came on outside the stadium, we were finding it hard enough to face Waqar and Wasim; how could we know what was to happen if we had walked off? I looked towards the dressing room, trying to catch the eye of Azhar, our captain, or Ashok Mankad, our manager. Kaka, as Mankad was fondly called, told us he didn't know what playing condition was to be used, so he asked us to continue batting.

In his book *Azharuddin – A Biography*, Harsha Bhogle, who was covering this match as a print journalist, recounts how Azhar himself didn't know what the playing conditions were and turned to the press box – which was next to the players' balcony – for comparative scores and if the press people knew what the playing conditions were. Asif Iqbal, the man responsible for the show, was seen running from door to door. Bhogle wrote that he asked the reserve umpire who would win if the match was to be called off, and he was told, 'I don't know, I will have to check the playing conditions.'

What made things suspicious was that the result of that match had no bearing on the final in two days' time. India and Pakistan had already qualified for it, so the result of the ongoing match was more open to manipulation than a more consequential encounter.

So we batted on under Kaka's instructions. Azhar told Bhogle that he wanted to call us back because he was concerned about our safety but he was overruled. Wickets fell as we batted in the dark – Kapil for a golden duck just after me – and in the end Prabhakar and More were tasked with getting 12 runs off the last over to be bowled by Waqar in pitch darkness. We lost by four runs, but this match only gathered notoriety once the world came to know what match-fixing was in 2000. For the peace of my mind and with no definitive evidence to the contrary, I still believe this was down to the unprofessional manner in which the game was conducted on the field. It's unfortunate that the umpires for that game received flak even though they had done the right thing by offering us light and the option to walk off. Since Sachin and I were not sure about the playing conditions, we did not. Had we batted till the end, we would have won the game.

Off the field, though, there used to be a lot of glamour in Sharjah. Film stars, pop stars and other famous and infamous faces would often be seen in the luxurious boxes. We were – at least I was – blissfully unaware of what might have gone on under the surface. All I knew back then was that India versus Pakistan was a big draw, which is why we were invited to Sharjah and to other exhibition matches over and over again.

The exhibition matches were played in a light-hearted vein but would witness spurts of intense competition, often on an individual level. Take the instance of Javed Miandad and Dilip Vengsarkar – both quite similar as people, which is why they were friendly off the field. However, in one such exhibition match on the 1989 tour, Waqar bowled a lovely outswinging yorker that pitched on the base of Vengsarkar's off stump and sent it cartwheeling. I was at the non-striker's end, and I saw Vengsarkar was a little shaken up by the rookie's excellent bowling.

I got out shortly after, and I was having tea with Vengsarkar when Miandad walked straight towards him. And without any pleasantries, Miandad told Vengsarkar, 'You have had a long career. There was only one thing missing: "b Waqar Younis". You have now achieved that too.'

Vengsarkar tried to ignore this taunt, but when needled further he told Miandad that he had just walked in to bat and didn't see the ball properly. Miandad would have nothing of it, and kept on insisting that the kid was a terrific bowler. 'He has done this to quite a few very good batsmen, so don't feel so bad,' Miandad said.

After Miandad left, Vengsarkar conceded that Waqar was indeed a damn good bowler.

Waqar was not the only young talent that emerged from those exhibition matches on that tour. The story of Tendulkar hitting Qadir out of the park is also quite well known, but I saw the best of Tendulkar in those matches when he played Wasim Akram. Perhaps Tendulkar played more freely on such occasions, considering these were not ODIs. Tendulkar versus Wasim with both at their prime is perhaps the best rivalry that never was. Those matches were not on TV, but from my ringside view I saw Tendulkar dominate Wasim. I remember how Mudassar Nazar observed during one such exhibition match – the best slog-overs bowler in the world was hit all over the park by Tendulkar quite effortlessly. Tendulkar will never boast openly, but he used to often wonder why other batsmen found Wasim so tough to play. I used to think, 'Because you are not like other batsmen, Sachin.'

Because Tendulkar had captured the imagination of the cricket world, and because I had had a good series, we would be recognized anywhere we went. I had seen a lot of Pakistan players wear a certain kind of sandal – especially Imran – and I had to buy them. So at the end of the tour, both of us went to a market in Peshawar. We reached a narrow street lined up on both sides with just sandal shops. As we looked in a few stores, word spread that we were there. The street soon filled up with hundreds of people, all gaping at us. I have mixed feelings about that experience. It was nice to see the effect we were having on people, and it was our first real experience of what it was like to be famous, but at the time I'd felt a little vulnerable because I had seen the hostility from Pakistan fans in Sharjah. Here, though, they just looked at us, two India cricketers, in awe. Nobody hassled us. I got my sandals, I liked them a lot, and I didn't have to pay for them.

6
THE 1996 WORLD CUP

THE 1996 WORLD Cup remains in memory as a missed opportunity. Imagine winning just two matches after beating a strong Pakistan team in familiar conditions and we could have been WC champions. Thankfully, M.S. Dhoni managed to do that fifteen years later; so that's some solace for those of us who were in the 1996 WC team.

Opportunity missed? Yes, but Indian cricket grabbed the opportunities that came with the 1996 World Cup to completely change its own economy.

*

It was Kerry Packer with the World Series in 1977, Lalit Modi with the IPL in 2008, but the game changer in the 1990s was Mark Mascarenhas and his TV company WorldTel. It took an outsider, an American with Indian origins, to actually tell us how much the game of cricket was worth and show the world its real value.

Holding hands with BCCI bigwigs Jagmohan Dalmiya and I.S. Bindra, Mascarenhas helped take the 1996 World Cup away from state broadcaster Doordarshan and brought private players in to take Indian cricket to people's homes.

His company WorldTel bid $10 million – $1.5 million more than the next highest bid – and agreed to pay $2.5 million up front.

This got the World Cup going, but nobody gave Mascarenhas a chance of recovering that money back.

But Mascarenhas was no fool; he threw the games open to all kinds of advertisers, found untapped markets, and the revenues from the World Cup went past $20 million.

For the first time in India, we had television crews from around the world producing a world-class cricket coverage.

There were commercial breaks between overs – another first. It helped that the Indian economy had opened itself to foreign investments and, therefore, there were international brands ready to pay handsome money just to be able to associate with India's favourite occupation – cricket.

The biggest beneficiaries were us, the players. Mascarenhas would also go on to become Sachin Tendulkar's agent. This was the first time we heard the term 'crore' mentioned in the context of cricket. After all, Mascarenhas had got Tendulkar a contract worth Rs 30 crore. As Ajay Jadeja used to say at that time, it was not just Tendulkar making the big money now.

Jadeja felt that Tendulkar had now drawn the line – with a crore being the benchmark to consider if you had signed up a star cricketer.

Now, not everyone could afford Tendulkar. So if they needed a cricketer and didn't have the budget for someone like Tendulkar, they would approach someone like a Jadeja.

Those smaller-budget companies, Jadeja felt, were bound to think, 'If Tendulkar is charging so much, Jadeja must be worth at least this much.' That amount was much smaller in comparison to Tendulkar's, but it was still a big jump from any amount we had made before.

Ajay Jadeja had become a significant commercial brand himself; because of his commercial success I realized that a smile not only opens doors but also treasure chests.

His popularity owed as much to his smile as it did to his batting and fielding. A few months before the 1996 World Cup, we had assembled in Bangalore for a training camp. Rahul Dravid was one of the probables. During one of our photo sessions for accreditation purposes, I told Jadeja, 'Jaad, if this guy gets selected for India, he is going to take your market away. Look at him – he is pretty good looking.'

Jadeja laughed and said, 'No chance. Look at him, he is so serious … and look how he is frowning. No way will he become popular. You need a smile to be loved by the fans.'

Jadeja was right about the smile but not about Dravid's popularity.

It was not just Tendulkar and Jadeja, though. Almost every player gained from the ensuing windfall. Wills and Four Square, the two major tobacco brands in India at the time, locked horns to draw mileage out of the 1996 World Cup. They went after our bats. All of us had bat contracts before, but now the scales changed. The two firms went to a whole new level with their offers.

As a result, the Indian squad for the 1996 World Cup got divided into two groups, the 'Wills' group and the 'Four Square' group. There was a lot of friendly banter about this in the team. Here were two rival tobacco companies fighting for space in Indian cricket, and the players enjoying the spoils. Some of us joked that tobacco was certainly not injurious to our health.

Around the same time, another originally tobacco man, Lalit Modi, was making plans for an 'intercity' league - but the traditional cricket administration was not ready for two mavericks yet.

Cricket had already taken a huge step forward with Mascarenhas and was dealing with the new world that he had brought in with WorldTel. One step at a time, it seemed, was the philosophy of the BCCI.

This intercity league, brainchild of Lalit Modi, finally came to fruition twelve years later. Maybe 1996 would have been too early for this concept. I think IPL in its T20 form came at the right time, and India was ready for it.

The cricket administration at the time was a bit like our team. We couldn't recover from the big win against Pakistan in the quarter-final of that 1996 World Cup. It is my firm belief that we lost the semi-final against Sri Lanka at Eden Gardens because we won that quarter-final against Pakistan.

Winning against Pakistan was such a big deal that we carried the hangover of the emotions spent for a few days and we just couldn't recover in time and be fresh mentally for the Sri Lanka game.

Having said that, the match against Pakistan was indeed an incredible one. One of the best I have played in.

The stage was set. A knockout WC match. Against our arch-rivals. In Bangalore. We would usually reach the ground very early. We took the first lap of the ground, warming up, about an hour and a half before the start of the match.

The stadium was already jam-packed. The noise the fans made was just unbelievable. As the Indian team was going through the pre-match routine, seeing the atmosphere around me, I was overcome by a strong feeling. I thought, 'You know what, we can't lose today. It's just not possible. The fan support is just too great, too unbelievable. Pakistan has to beat them first, then beat us.'

I'm sure that's how Pakistan must have felt every time we played them in Sharjah.

We batted first. Our batting was okay until Jadeja tore into Waqar Younis towards the end of our innings. His innings made what was the eventual winning difference.

Even though we set a target of 287, a big score in fifty-overs cricket at that time, the way Pakistan came out chasing it, it shook any illusion that we had enough runs on the board.

This quality of the Pakistan team is what made me such a big fan of their cricket throughout my playing days.

Even though Imran Khan had retired by then and they were not quite the force they used to be, it was still a very strong team and they were favourites to win the WC. Their openers, Aamer Sohail and Saeed Anwar, came at us like wounded tigers.

Their body language was extremely aggressive and thus began a spirited run chase.

They were right in our faces all the time. It became quite clear that even after putting up a big score we could not take things for granted one bit. The Indian teams of the post-2010 era are incredibly lucky – they get to play a Pakistan team that's only a shadow of the team of the '80s and '90s.

I remember standing at mid-off and mid-on for Javagal Srinath and Venkatesh Prasad and seeing the tension and anxiety on their faces as Sohail and Anwar went after them, hitting even their good-length balls on the up for scorching boundaries. I kept urging them to bowl fuller and try and swing the ball. I felt that was the only way to beat the bat and get a wicket. If we bowled length or short of length, even at pace those guys were going to hammer us.

My advice fell on deaf ears, though – the atmosphere had got to everyone. The adrenaline was too high for them to listen to reason. They were perhaps thinking that fours would become sixes if they bowled too full in their search for swing.

That evening, I realized it was easier for me to advise them than to actually do what they were doing. I was not in their shoes, bowling on a flat pitch to two dangerous batsmen on a massive stage in front of a packed stadium. Maybe that's why they played safe, hoping that the batsmen would eventually make a mistake.

As it turned out, it was Sohail who made a mistake, and with every mistake that followed, the crowd kept finding its voice, and we kept coming back. Javed Miandad, playing in what was to be the final ODI of his career, was struggling too but he hung in till the end, hoping that the 'Miandad magic' would come back to him. Right towards the end, after we got Saleem Malik out, when we began to think the match was done, in came Rashid Latif and hit one of our seamers for a six over long-on. I remember thinking, at that moment, this Pakistan team is like a lizard – try and kill it, the tail still has a life of its own.

In a sense, it took a lot from us, both mentally and physically, to beat them. It was a pretty close game – at least it felt like one – in a charged-up atmosphere. It was going to be a long way down from that high. After the game, Miandad, his sixth World Cup finally behind him, spent more time in our dressing room than his own, just chilling with us, soaking in the occasion. I found that both strange and nice.

That night, as India's young lot of cricketers, we went out to enjoy the night life of Bangalore. Jadeja, of course, was our tour leader. I will never forget the reactions we got wherever we went that night. We were like gods that had descended from the heavens and walked into their establishment. It was a heady feeling. We of course, soaked in all the love we got.

The next few days were spent in Bangalore, at the Taj Westend Hotel. Everybody spent their time unwinding, savouring the sweet feeling of having beaten Pakistan. After that game, it became steadily easier for India to beat Pakistan, but this was still the '90s, and it was very uncommon then.

When it was time to turn up for the semi-final, a lot of us had not recovered from the euphoria of the previous game. Ajit Wadekar, our team manager, sensed that.

Wadekar carried an image of a happy-go-lucky character who bumbled his way through life. In reality, I found out he was the exact opposite, especially when in a position of responsibility – be it as the Indian captain or as an employee at the State Bank of India where he rose in the organization to reach one of the top positions that any Indian Test cricketer held in the corporate world.

There was something about Wadekar. It is no coincidence that the famous 1971 triumphs in the West Indies and England came under him. He was one of those people who felt Indian cricket should be second to none. When he was made India coach, it was a surprise for everyone. He had been out of the game for a while, and at first didn't seem physically ready to go through the rigours that a hands-on coach needs to. After a few days, though, he got himself fit enough to give us a 100 catches a day.

More importantly, Wadekar became the boss of the team. Indian cricket teams are generally run by the captain and one or two seniors. The coach is often like a prop on the stage, happy to keep his job and not rock the boat. Not Wadekar, though. For the first time in my career I knew who was taking important decisions and he was happy to accept responsibility for that. He found it hard to accept defeats on earlier tours, like the one to South Africa in 1992-93. You could see that it hurt him, personally.

Wadekar was the first Indian coach who made sure everybody was making the most of the practice sessions. He didn't let anyone take it easy for even a minute. For example, after the batsmen had finished their knock in the nets, they were immediately sent to relentless fielding drills: taking catches and attacking the ball when it was hit at you and then trying to hit the stumps directly. He was smart – he knew what Indian cricket lacked and made sure he was going to do something about it.

Importantly, Wadekar knew that the Indian team had the tendency to relax after tasting some success. I remember once when after winning a match, we were having some fun on the flight. That evening in the team meeting at the hotel, he shouted at us unexpectedly, 'What do you think? You have won the tournament or something? What was happening in the flight? What kind of behaviour was that?'

Before the semi-final against Sri Lanka, he sensed something similar and he called for a team meeting. It went on for quite long; Wadekar did most of the talking. Once he was done, Mohammad Azharuddin, the captain, spoke a few words. Although that meeting lasted an hour or so, around fifty minutes were spent on how to contain their openers Romesh Kaluwitharana and Sanath Jayasuriya. The duo had decimated us in a league match earlier in the tournament, chasing down 272 without any fuss. They had reduced Manoj Prabhakar to bowling off-spin, hastening the end of his career.

Imagine our surprise, then, when we got both out in the first over in the semi-final. I caught Kaluwitharana for a golden duck at third man off Srinath, and his new-ball partner Venkatesh Prasad caught Jayasuriya. Now we didn't know what to do. Like Abhimanyu in Mahabharata, we had trained ourselves to get to the target in the 'chakravyuh' but didn't prepare ourselves about getting out of it.

We relaxed, in a fashion typical of the cricket we played in the '90s. If you look at our jubilation after getting Kaluwitharana and Jayasuriya out, it was as if we had won the World Cup. We basically took the eye off the ball, and Aravinda de Silva made us pay for it. Sri Lanka ended up scoring 251.

In the chase, Tendulkar and I had a 90-run partnership, and at no point did we think there were any real demons in the pitch.

Now, a pitch should not change in ten minutes. But that's what wickets do; a few fell quickly and the demons woke up.

Kumar Dharmasena bowled an off-break to Azhar that pitched outside off and ended up with Kaluwitharana down the leg side – he had to collect it chest high. It was called a wide; I will never forget Dharmasena's smile – to me it was the smile of the devil, but he had perhaps realized that the match was theirs now; they would go to Lahore for the finals, not India.

Apart from Dharmasena, they had three more spinners – Muttiah Muralitharan, Jayasuriya and de Silva, if needed. With Tendulkar gone and with him a couple of other top-order batsmen back in the pavilion, we also knew in our hearts it was all over.

Since that night, there's been a lot of debate about our decision to bowl first after winning the toss. There have been accusations of match-fixing, accusations that Azhar went against what was decided in the team meeting. At its most charitable, the criticism held us guilty of misreading the pitch and going against the wisdom of having runs on the board in a big match.

Truth be told, there was no devious motive. I can vouch for that. The consensus in the team meeting was that Sri Lanka had been chasing extremely well, and they had walloped us when batting second in the league games. We didn't want them to chase. The approach was a little negative, but they had been riding this incredible wave of chasing and winning that we wanted to put them off their comfort zone.

In one-day cricket the pitch doesn't matter that much. I remember I didn't even look at the pitch. At least to us in that meeting before the match, batting second didn't seem like a shocking or a radical decision. We bowled first at Lord's in 1990, when Graham Gooch scored 333 in the first innings – you could call that a ridiculous decision. But we didn't have any such feeling about this one. This wasn't a blunder. A fair criticism would be to say that we didn't play to our strengths – we were so afraid of Sri Lanka's ability to chase that we didn't want to give them that opportunity. And when Sachin and I were batting, the pitch didn't look that unplayable. Given the same situation again, I concede that my vote would be to bat first.

After the match we all had our heads in our hands. The dressing room at the Eden Gardens was quiet and gloomy. Srinath was trying to get my attention; he pointed to Sunil Gavaskar who had also joined us. He was sobbing. I didn't know what to make of it.

We were all sitting quietly, and I could feel a set of eyes again on me; it was Navjot Singh Sidhu this time. Only with his hands and eyes he was telling me: 'See, I told you so.' He was perhaps the only one in the team who had felt strongly about us batting first and had openly opposed the idea of chasing. (He was a good reader of pitches, by the way.)

So we went back to our hotel like lambs to slaughter. Angry fans vandalized the bus. Normally, at the Eden Gardens, we would take a left when we would come out of the stadium but that night we had to turn right to avoid angry fans who had lined up on the familiar route to pelt stones at our bus. A common reaction of fans then – it was no big deal for us.

As a sportsman, you'd want to forget such a night as soon as possible. So at the hotel, we gathered in one room – Tendulkar, Jadeja, myself and a couple of others. Even in domestic cricket or at the school level, whenever we were knocked out early, we tried to laugh it away. That night, we were possibly trying to do the same. We were just talking generally, sort of telling each other that nobody had died, when Vinod Kambli walked in.

Kambli, who'd remained not out in our run chase, had broken down in the middle as our innings and our World Cup dream fell apart. Seeing Kambli come in, Jadeja just got up and let it rip. He said, 'The only guy who has felt about this defeat is Dessee [Kambli's nickname, after Desmond Haynes]. All of us have felt nothing. Look how he was crying out there.'

Jadeja was upset at Kambli's exhibition of emotion. It was rare to see Jadeja that angry. In Kambli's defence, it was perhaps the way the match ended that made him become emotional in the middle. The Eden Gardens crowd had disrupted play; the match referee Sir Clive Lloyd had eventually awarded the match to the Lankans.

It's the highest-capacity ground in India, but the Eden Gardens can be a strange place. It was here, early in my career, that I realized that the fanfare doesn't mean much. I remember one Challenger Trophy game there when I got a hundred and won the match for my team, and the crowd stood up in the stands to applaud me. Now, the Challenger Trophy is a short tournament with consecutive matches at the same venue. So the next day, at the same ground, in front of the same people, I struggled and played a typically slow, Sanjay Manjrekar innings. When I was dismissed, while walking back to the pavilion I could hear abuse and feel things hurled at me. In a matter of twenty-four hours, I had turned villain.

Many years later, when the local boy Sourav Ganguly was dropped from the team and Rahul Dravid was made captain, the Eden Gardens crowd supported South Africa and urged them to win. It was a sad sight, but I wasn't surprised. I know the 60,000-odd people at Eden Gardens do not represent the whole city of Kolkata, but that day I lost a bit of respect for its cricket-loving people. Thankfully, it hasn't come in my way of loving Bengali music, especially Rabindra Sangeet. I consider Bengali food one of the best cuisines in the world. I love Kolkata, the city. I just wish the cricket fans there had a better understanding of the game than just following it passionately.

Just like them, we too wanted to win that World Cup. We'd made it to the semi-final and we too felt it was a brilliant chance of winning it for the second time. I think most of us felt we won the World Cup when we beat Pakistan in the quarter-final. We were walking on clouds. We had a tremendous record playing at home, but we got ahead of ourselves. Those were the weaknesses we had as a team. Later teams became temperamentally much stronger. Under M.S. Dhoni's captaincy, all these weaknesses disappeared.

It was great to be in the home World Cup of 1996, to take Kaluwitharana's catch at third man and have a hundred thousand people celebrate with me, but as players we tend to get used to the atmosphere at international matches. We could feel the expectations and the passion of the fans, like when we took the lap of Chinnaswamy Stadium before the Pakistan match. At other times we develop a bit of a tunnel vision about what's going on in the field. So it never got to a stage where I imagined or visualized what winning the World Cup would mean to the fans, or to us.

We rarely get to know the fans well. They are like a blur of heads you see in the background of a still action picture. We played in grounds where tens of thousands would come in and create this almighty noise. Often we would go into a crunch match having had a pretty animated team meeting, reinforcing that we needed to keep egging each other on in the field and keep the intensity up. And then the next day when the match would start it used to be so noisy that we could not hear each other even ten feet away. All that planning and discussion about spurring each other on would come to nought. We had to just resign to the atmosphere, and then it would be just hand gestures to communicate with each other.

When we played badly, coaches and team managers would never fail to tell us, 'You have to think about the fans ... how much they want us to win. Let's do it for them.' We used to find it difficult to connect with that emotion. We all lived in a bit of a bubble.

But to be fair, that disconnect also becomes a strength for a player. To not be aware of how big a game is, or how much hinges on its outcome, or how many people are watching him play. I have always felt that players don't feel it as much. Not that they don't care about it – this is only their defence mechanism.

In a way, we train ourselves in such a way that our defeats end up hurting our fans more than they hurt us. I should know – I was a fan once. When Javed Miandad beat India in Sharjah with the last-ball six off Chetan Sharma, I couldn't take it. That match finished quite late, and by that time it was getting dark in Mumbai, a time of day I find quite depressing. So the combination of the defeat and the general time of the day left me quite sad. I stepped out of my house, met some of my friends – they were into cricket too, so they were sad as well. That night was too depressing.

As a player, though, I don't remember ever feeling as sad as we did that night in Kolkata. We just took the flight the next day to go home. We didn't call each other two days later to make sure we were not depressed. The fans must understand that we do care, but we are required to train ourselves not to care too much.

This is what Dhoni changed remarkably as a captain. He downplayed everything, the importance, the significance and the rewards at the end of a match. Having conducted tosses during big games, I have seen Dhoni make a deliberate attempt to just be cool and quiet. Some captains are slightly tense or charged up. It's not that Dhoni doesn't feel it, it's just that he knows how to handle it. Often, he loves to indulge in a chat about non-cricketing stuff at such times, just something to take his mind off the enormity of the game and simplify it. That's what champions do. That's how India became world champions again in 2011.

7
STRUGGLES

TWENTY-FIVE YEARS IS a long time but it all came back to me in one forward-defensive shot. I've hardly played any cricket post retirement, but in 2014, a quarter of a century after I had toured Pakistan, I padded up to face Wasim Akram for a TV show we were doing on biomechanics. It was during India's tour of England. The shoot was for a segment on what biomechanics experts brought to cricket. I was going to face an over from Wasim in the indoor nets, during which my technique and body movements would be recorded and studied by a biomechanics expert.

In came Wasim, the same easy run-up, the energy through the crease, the quick arm. I let my natural batting style take over, and moved forward to the first couple of deliveries. There it was – in a flash it all came back to me. It was 1989, the memorable tour of Pakistan played out all over again in front of my eyes as I got on to the front foot and played Wasim comfortably. The words of Imran Khan, the generous Pakistan captain, rang in my ears: 'Why did you play Richard Hadlee off the back foot?' he had asked me after I struggled on the 1990 tour of New Zealand, a year after I had done well in Pakistan. 'You played Wasim so well in Pakistan because you played him off the front foot.'

Later, the biomechanics expert came back with his analysis. They had installed a camera right on top of me, inside the net. The findings revealed an exaggerated movement of my back foot towards the off stump leaving me off balance, thereby hampering my strokeplay on the off side, especially the cut shot. I was just getting too close to balls to unleash the cut shot. This man was not even a cricket expert – he only studied my body movements – and even he could see I was doing something wrong. I was not balanced.

That front-foot forward movement of 1989, without any self-doubt, with the mind free of any demons … oh, it felt so good. The ability to cut and cover-drive to keep the runs coming – it seemed from a time so long ago. I wondered if a biomechanics expert or a personal batting coach could have helped me during the torture that the last five years of my cricketing career were. The years of struggle that defined my Test career: 21 Tests for an average of 29, after a promising start of 16 matches for an average of 48, with only two of those matches played at home.

Then I rationalized. One tip from a biomechanics expert or a personal coach could not have possibly ignited the spark that I was waiting for. It couldn't have been that easy. My problems were deeper. How could a biomechanics expert change the person I was? There is a Marathi saying: '*Swabhavala aushad nahi*.' There is no medicine for nature.

As was my nature, I kept working on my technique. A bit of a perfectionist looking for ways to eliminate flaws that had infiltrated my game. Every day I went to the nets to try to sort some issue out, but I felt like a boat with holes: I covered one, and water would enter through the other. I kept hoping I would find the missing piece to make it all fall in place. A big score that would secure my place in the Indian team. And then I could just bat without worrying about failure and the various technical issues. Just watch the ball and react without thinking, like I did in Pakistan in 1989. Bat the way batting is meant to be.

*

When you are in form, there isn't much to say or write about. It is like being on autopilot. Good things happen without even trying. After the ball is halfway towards the boundary you realize you have just played a beautiful cover drive right from the middle of the bat. It's a brilliant feeling.

People say you can psyche yourself into feeling that way every time, even when you are out of form, that you can visualize yourself being in top form. Not me. I could never fool myself into feeling on top of the world when my confidence was at rock bottom. I was too rational and too much of a sceptic to be able to do that.

That analytical side of me had made be believe in the first place that I was good enough to be out there. When I went to Pakistan, for example, I knew I could handle Wasim Akram and Abdul Qadir. This came from the deep-rooted self-confidence from having scored a hundred against West Indies in the West Indies. Even when I had made my debut against that all-conquering side, there were no demons from any recent bad experiences against them.

My first Test, the big jump from first-class cricket to international cricket, was at Feroz Shah Kotla in Delhi. Dilip Vengsarkar, the

India captain then, was feeling a little let down by other batsmen who didn't quite stand up to the West Indies quicks. He always supported me, thought I had what it took, but he wanted some reassurance before giving me the big break.

'Ghatta, you'll do it, no, if you get a chance?' Vengsarkar asked me. I used to be called Ghatta by my Mumbai team-mates. It means 'tight' in Marathi. I used to carry myself very tight and stiff, they thought.

West Indies were imposing, but my slate with them was clean. So I said, '*Mee zaaoon ubhaa raheen* [I will stand up to them, don't worry].'

Vengsarkar said, 'What's the point of just standing up to them? Who will get the runs?'

I did not have an answer to that. I really didn't. I knew I had the defence but I was not sure yet if I had the shots against this kind of top-class fast bowling. We were bowled out for 75 in the first innings, and I was retired hurt for 10 in the second, but not before I had faced 63 balls. I drew a lot of confidence from that little exposure. That I could face up to these guys in an intense Test-match atmosphere with a degree of comfort.

The next time I batted in a Test again was in the West Indies, in Barbados, and without thinking about it too much, I had found an answer to Vengsarkar's question. I had found a way to score runs, 108 of them. My first Test hundred. I left the bouncers alone because nobody hooked then, and they bowled about three every over. I remember cutting a lot, hitting short balls over the slips or through point. I also went on to the back foot to work balls through square leg a lot. It would get me only a single on most occasions, but it was an effective shot. It could get me off strike. Kiran More later told me how much he liked that shot.

I brought up the hundred with a straight drive when Courtney Walsh pitched one up. During the innings, I drove Curtly Ambrose over extra cover on the up, and I remember feeling, 'Shit, that's great. I can even play this shot against these guys.' I was an international player now. My mind had the evidence right there to think of myself as an international-class player.

When I came back, I went to the Wankhede Stadium for a session at the nets. It is usually lively there early in the morning. I was facing the Mumbai seamers. The first time they pitched short to me, I was in position on the back foot well before the ball arrived. They seemed gentle seam bowlers to me now.

I was feeling great about my game, and I carried it into the tour of Pakistan where I scored a double-century and a century, top-scoring with 569 runs at an average of 95 in four Tests. I did all this without having to think too much about my game. Reverse swing was a bigger threat back then because the swing was more pronounced, and Pakistan were masters of it, but I got all those runs not knowing a thing about the shiny side and the rough side on the old ball. All that came much later in my life, when Sachin Tendulkar planted the seed in my head in one Ranji game about how you can get early indication of which way the ball was going to swing by watching the two sides of the ball closely. Until then I just watched the ball as a whole – I watched it till late and reacted late.

That was my strength. I played the ball late, never committed, and hence swing was never difficult for me to play. With Wasim, I could tell how the ball was going to behave by just watching his wrist. The ball travels the twenty-two yards in a fraction of a second, but there is still enough time for a trained batsman to see what is happening.

When we went into the last Test of that tour, we were put in on a green top in Sialkot. I was in great form and top-scored in the first innings with 72. It was a Test affected by rain, and there was no chance of a result when we batted the second time around. Our coach Chandu Borde noticed that I didn't take a knock that morning. He asked me if I wasn't going to do it, and I said no. I got out for four.

Borde said to me, 'It always helps if you take a knock.'

This was me just taking things for granted a bit, being casual about a Test innings, something I never saw Sachin Tendulkar do.

I was now being spoken of as the future of Indian batting, and I had earned that tag through runs in difficult conditions and against the two best attacks in the world. When I came back from the West Indies, I got a lot of attention, being the only success story on that tour. My mother and my family had kept clippings from all the newspapers. I read them and dismissed them because the praise was exaggerated. I knew I was good but not that good.

However, during this phase people close to me also saw me get a bit cocky, not necessarily on the field but off it. I would throw tantrums if things didn't go as per plan. I might have taken some Ranji and company games in this period lightly since it didn't matter how many runs I got in them. Tendulkar, again, was a study in contrast: Whenever he was out there in public view, he always gave his best no matter the magnitude of the game.

Brimming with self-confidence, I also enjoyed making others look small by exposing their weaknesses. In one inter-company match in Hyderabad, as captain I went out of my way to target Mohammad Azharuddin, now the India captain. I wanted everyone to see his weakness as a batsman, and how I was the smart one to expose it despite his other exceptional gifts. I learnt later that Azhar was unhappy with me for what I did. I had developed a habit of getting under people's skin.

Captaining gave me a great high right from the time I led my school to its first Giles Shield title. Surely there was nothing wrong with exposing an opposition player's weakness? Then, again, did I really need to do that to an India team-mate in a nondescript company match no one cared about? My sister fleetingly mentioned to me during this time that I came across as a bit arrogant in an interview she had watched on TV.

Today, I am a bit older and wiser. Whatever little success I have had in the media and in broadcasting, I have never let that get to my head. Back then, though, I was on top of the world.

*

When we went to Australia for a gruelling four-month tour in 1991-92, to play five Tests, a triangular ODI series and the World Cup, I was upbeat and really looking forward to the trip. I knew I was going to do really well there. I had the game for it. I was told I was a good player of pace and the short ball. I had also just been named the Man of the Series in the ODI series that welcomed South Africa back to cricket after the apartheid boycott.

I remember a conversation with Shivlal Yadav, who had a good record in Australia despite its reputation for being a graveyard for finger spinners. I was a bit concerned about being away from home for so long, and his response was, 'Homesick in Australia? What?' He seemed to have had a great time there. I intended to do the same.

I was with my friends Tendulkar and Venkatapathy Raju. Another friend, Vinod Kambli, was to join us for the World Cup.

Life could not have been better at that stage. There we were, in a wonderful country, blissfully unaware – at least I was – that this tour could make or break careers.

What's more, at the start of the tour I helped us win a side game, a 50-over match. Our next assignment was a first-class match against New South Wales in Lismore, just before the first Test. Feeling I was in good form, I didn't take the match seriously even though New South Wales fielded Mark Taylor, the Waugh twins, Geoff Lawson, Greg Matthews, Mike Whitney and Michael Bevan.

I played loose shots in both the innings to get out on low scores to a really quick bowler, Wayne Holdsworth. Vengsarkar caught hold of me, and said, 'You batted like you were carrying on from the previous innings.' We lost the 'side' game by an innings.

The twin failures didn't bother me one bit. I couldn't wait for the first Test to start and resume my terrific international form. Cricket, though, had other plans in mind. I scored only 197 runs in nine innings. It was a strange series because I still faced the third-most balls in that Indian side. I reached 25 five times but couldn't convert even one of those starts into a fifty. I never felt out of form, but kept finding ways to get out after getting my eye in. I even ran myself out, on 45 in Adelaide when we threatened to pull off a 372-run chase in the fourth innings but fell short by just 38 runs.

It was that run-out that rankled me the most. I had just started having visions of winning the match for India with a hundred. I was run out six times on that tour. I didn't know it at the time, but this was down to my lack of peak fitness. Mumbai cricket was more about skills; fitness was an afterthought. My legs weren't strong enough to carry the burden of a long Australian tour. Sometimes at the non-striker's end, I would be preoccupied with how I was batting and not concentrate on the running, but mostly it was the tired and weak legs. I would take off for a quick run only to discover I didn't have the explosive strength in my legs to complete that run. And the big and soft outfields of Australia expose any weakness in your legs quite easily.

The fascinating part of that tour, though, was that my self-confidence never took a dive. The positivity in my mind was unshakeable. Excitement kept me up at nights. I would just lie in the bed thinking how all this was going to change next morning when I'd get a hundred, and how good that feeling would be. I felt exactly how I did as an eleven-year-old, unable to sleep, thinking of the certain Giles Shield century, and the excitement of seeing my name in the newspapers. Coming back to form was an inevitability in my mind. Going into the last Test in Perth, the excitement was almost unbearable. 'Fastest pitch in the world. What a place to get a hundred and come back,' I told myself.

I got 31 and 8 in that match.

My self-confidence began to erode slowly now. The first response was to take the frustration out in the dressing room. Often, I would blame those batting with me for my dismissal, especially in run-out situations. I would call them names to let off steam. I was told later to watch my language because whatever one said could get conveyed in a different way to the other person. It was an important lesson: The dressing room, although private, was still a very public space.

Right through that tour, I played exactly the same way. I didn't change anything. Much of this was because my confidence was still intact, and because I was getting out in a variety of ways – so there was no specific weakness to work on. Also, I was consciously not overreacting to failure – there was more the history of success that was etched in my mind until then.

On the 1990 tour of New Zealand, at a nets session Kapil Dev remarked to me that I was moving too far across when trying to get in line with the ball. 'Your leg stump shows,' he said. Manoj Prabhakar countered him, saying my back lift was quite low so I would be able to adjust; it's no big deal, he said.

But I reacted to Kapil's observation. I wish I had the clarity of Prabhakar, but instead I moved my guard to four inches outside the leg stump. In the Auckland Test I thought I left Danny Morrison alone outside off only to find the ball crashing into my off stump. My instinct had not kept up with my changed technique.

During that phase, Vengsarkar told me not to bother about technique too much and just go out and score runs. I managed to grind my way to a century against Zimbabwe immediately after that tour, but the obsessive analyst in me had now been woken up.

Frank Tyson used to do a lot of coaching at the Cricket Club of India in Mumbai at that time. So I sought him out. He noticed that as I got ready to face the ball my back lift would remain low. I was picking my bat up with just my wrists, and not arms. Therefore my bat wouldn't get high enough to play the short and bouncing deliveries. Someone like Brian Lara, on the other hand, would have his bat close to the height of the short ball even as he prepared to face it. From there, it was just about coming down on the ball as opposed to start raising the bat with the ball halfway down the pitch.

Tyson's logic convinced me. In the Zimbabwe and South Africa tours that followed, people would have seen a distinct change in the way I lifted the bat as I prepared to face the ball. This change didn't bring any dramatic turnaround I was hoping for; I got a 100 versus Zimbabwe, a match-saving one, but my batting struggles had not diminished. I was batting unnaturally now. Like how English batsmen do.

In Australia, I looked good even when failing, but in South Africa I was well and truly out of sorts. My whole game was about reacting naturally to the ball not knowing what was happening to my bat. Now I was focusing on the bat more than the ball.

Colleagues like Vengsarkar sometimes mocked my changed back lift, but out of respect, perhaps, he didn't press the matter. He knew I was serious about this change, that I was convinced it was going to solve all my problems.

I was dropped from the side when India were hammering England and Zimbabwe at home. I was given a chance to impress the selectors in a side game for Rest of India against the touring England side in 1993, in Visakhapatnam.

Facing Phil DeFreitas in that game, I punched one down the ground and shouted 'no', expecting mid-on to slide sideways and stop the ball, like it had happened in South Africa for the last two months. Here, Phil Tufnell started to run after the ball and soon gave up the chase. It had suddenly all become easy again, at home and against an average England side. Even when I was out of form, I scored a fluent 96 without any trouble. India, though, just slammed England in the Tests. There was no need for a new batsman.

Had I played that series, I might have got that big score that I was looking for. England at home were perfect opponents to come back into form, like Azhar did at Eden Gardens in 1996, but I was rightly dropped. That patch of low scores justified my exclusion.

I got my chance later against Sri Lanka and then West Indies. In those series I scored two 60s, a 50, a 40, a 30, but, again, that innings which I hoped would turn it all around eluded me. In Mumbai, against a red-hot West Indies attack of Courtney Walsh,

Kenny Benjamin and Cameron Cuffy, I scored half-centuries to rescue India from 99 for 5 and 88 for 5, setting up the win. In the second innings, my anxiousness got the better of me. I had had a big partnership with Tendulkar, India were in the clear, but wickets were falling and I was on 66 with only three wickets in hand. I was eager. I wanted that hundred, and I did something uncharacteristic. I played a lofted shot off Walsh *in a Test match,* and picked out the tall Cuffy at mid-on.

After the match, Sunil Gavaskar tapped me on my head and only said, 'Tchah.' He knew I had missed a great opportunity to get a hundred. I could sense that a lot of people around me wanted me to do well and make a strong comeback. In their books I was still a fine batsman. I was disappointed, of course, but I had still played two crucial innings in a Test win, and it was a very nice feeling.

After that Test, the late Hemant Waingankar, a real well-wisher of Mumbai cricket and its players, took me to the city's famous Siddhivinayak Temple to thank the gods, to sort of pray that the worst was over now. Anil Joshi, who has been my loyalist for over thirty-five years, was there too. Hemant even got me something to wear around my neck for good luck. In the next Test, at Nagpur, I got scores of 0 and 5. I removed that thing from my neck immediately.

Something more significant happened. I got out fending off a short ball from Benjamin. That hurt my pride. People considered me one of the best players of fast bowling, especially the short ball, and now I had got out to it, that too on an Indian pitch. I began to think, 'Is this another little chink entering my game?'

I analysed video replays of that dismissal, and it irked me that my weight was back as I gloved the short ball. It made it appear as if I was scared of the short ball, which I was not. I had conquered that fear of the short ball when the other Benjamin, Winston, had hit me on the eye in my debut Test. There I had got into a great position to play that short ball but it beat me off the seam. There was no technical issue, no fear, the weight was not going back. The ball just beat me.

In those days, I wore a helmet without a grille and it was a nasty injury. The ball had hit me straight on the eye. I had to be stapled up. I made a comeback immediately, against the same guys in a side game because I wanted to prove myself. I represented the Board President's XI against the West Indies in Visakhapatnam on one of the worst pitches I've played on. They bounced me again, but I always kept moving forward. One length ball rose and hit me on the helmet grille – the grille flew off. I had incorporated it as part of my protective gear after my facial injury on my debut. I still fought and survived, and went to the West Indies and scored a century.

So, fear was not my problem. My problem was the weight going back and the position of the gloves in front of the face. It was almost beyond your control. You know you can't be getting your gloves that high. As the fast bowler runs in, you tell yourself to keep your hands low and try to get out of the way of the short ball. You are well protected in case you get hit, I would tell myself. In that phase, though, I just could not prevent those hands from getting in front of my face. They seemed to have a mind of their own. It was like I was willing for one thing to happen but something else would happen. I was down in the dumps now, especially on the 1996 tour of England. This was not just about failures – I was getting out to the short ball just like the batsmen I enjoyed targeting as captain.

During that tour, I went up to the media centre to meet Gavaskar, who was there as a commentator. He advised me to get into a position to hook or pull the moment I saw the ball coming in short, and to leave it alone if it was too high. It was good advice because it got you to look at the short ball as one to attack – like you would a spinner's short ball. Because the intention is to attack, you are in a good position to leave it too.

The advice didn't work for me, though. I could get into good positions on occasion, but at other times the hands would still come up to fend.

The analyst in me also thinks maybe it's all due to that injury I kept to myself and didn't tell anyone about – the stress fracture on my lower back. Vishwas Raut, a well-known orthopaedist who incidentally was on that 1989 tour to Pakistan as team doctor, had diagnosed it but it wasn't paralysing or serious enough to make me unfit to play; I would have to just manage somehow, he'd said.

In my latter years as a player, I would get a rub-down from the physiotherapist just as I went in to bat so that my lower back could become more supple. Else it would stiffen up and hinder my reflexes.

But here's the thing about fitness. When you are young, you react quickly. The moment the ball was short, I would wait till the last moment before reacting, and then I'd either duck or sway. As I grew older, this movement became slower. This brought some vulnerability in my play against fast and short bowling and unfortunately it started to bother me mentally. The moment the ball was pitched short, something inside me would make me get my gloves up to protect my face. Was it my facial injury on my debut that was triggering this instinct?

It was through sheer grit that I had conquered this immediately after my debut, a time when the instinct to protect my face should have been at its strongest. I remember managing to rein it in through my sheer self-confidence at the time. Now that I was older and filled with self-doubt, was that protective instinct raising its head again after so many years?

Players such as Steve Waugh, who had issues with the short ball, would just drop the hands the moment they saw the ball short. They didn't mind getting hit. M.S. Dhoni did that in England in 2014. You can hurt your body by this approach, but in most cases, you don't get out.

I guess I was too proud a batsman to do that. I was self-conscious; I was not willing to look ugly. I wanted also to get good-looking runs. I was not ready to be an ugly survivor. It was all about perfection, right?

That is why I admire greats like Steve Waugh, even Brian Lara. They were okay to look ordinary for a while despite their stature and reputation in the game to eventually play a great innings.

They focused on the final goal of getting runs and winning matches for their team. But I – I had to look good while getting there. That was my problem. My natural game was like a very sophisticated fine-tuned machinery that would tolerate no tampering. So every time I tried to make even the slightest of changes, it felt like too much of an adjustment mentally, and my whole game got out of sync.

Often it introduced new flaws. When I took Gavaskar's advice, to get into a position to hook every time somebody pitched short, it meant I had to make an exaggerated movement towards off stump and sometimes outside off. For me this was a big deal. Many batsmen make such changes without any fuss, but for me it was a big deal – to steer away from my natural game.

I also thought I'd managed fine with my original technique, so I didn't commit myself too much towards making this change.

But now that the virus had entered the system, I began obsessing about it – I was making very subtle changes almost every day. Even the keenest observers of my game would have seen nothing amiss, but there I was, making small but significant modifications to my game to get it in perfect harmony.

It was perhaps around that time that Ajit Wadekar showed me an article written by Raju Bharatan. He wrote: 'Sanjay Manjrekar's game is going from one weakness to another.' I agreed completely with him.

Interestingly, the fault spotted by the biomechanics expert in 2014 was something Navjot Sidhu had made a passing comment about during my days of struggle, but I hadn't given it much consideration. (The Sidhu of those days, by the way, was nothing like the Sidhu we see on TV nowadays. He was a serious man, generally quiet, but an astute observer of the game.)

My front foot was moving across towards the off stump along with my left hand far too early – it meant I was getting close to balls that were wide of the off stump too. So, in my head I never saw those balls as wide balls outside off to be square-cut for four, like I did in West Indies and Pakistan. It meant that my biggest ally, the square cut, the stroke that had seen me through all my travails against tough oppositions, had deserted me.

With my main weapon lost, it became even more of an effort to score runs. This began to take a toll on me: spending so much time at the crease and not getting runs. Mentally, it would exhaust me. It began to show in my behaviour. After my comeback series against West Indies in 1994-95, I was not picked for the triangular ODI series in New Zealand, and I had to go back to playing Ranji Trophy because the road of any international comeback was through domestic cricket.

When I captained Mumbai against Maharashtra in Solapur in early 1995, I was an angry, frustrated 'India discard'. My pet peeve in domestic cricket has always been the umpiring. Coming back

ight: The first year of my transition
om cricketer to commentator.

ottom left: Photo shoot in
loonreach. This is where I spent
ne most eventful years of my life.

ottom right: Always happy to stand
as wicket-keeper. Loved keeping
fter batting.

Helmet with grill became a part of me and my batting after the facial injury.

At Worli seaface for a photo shoot by a Kolkata-based newspaper.

The tour that changed my life. The Mumbai University team of 1984. Also featuring Rajdeep Sardesai (in the shirt with the 'X' sign on it).

ith Dilip Vengsarkar in West Indies. I owe ilip great gratitude for backing me when mattered.

Two Podar College products at the international level. I can visualize V.S. Patil smiling from the heavens seeing this photograph.

y fifth birthday. Was gifted a toy car at was immediately put in a showcase. ot to be touched, only admired.

Vijay Manjrekar in an ad for Ovomalt.

Top: Vizzy Trophy function 1984/85. M.G. Ramachandran presenting me the medal. I was captain of West Zone university team. We won that year.

Above: Richard Hadlee loved me. For being his 400th. This was a private photo for MRF, our sponsors.

Below: Hated official functions where we had to wear blazer and tie, etc. Sachin and I always hung around together. We preferred being on our own than mingle. Very unsocial.

Bottom: My father's benefit match in 1972 in Hubli. Great turnout of players. Rohan Kanhai came all the way from West Indies. But my father didn't make enough money from the game.

Above: The Mumbai coterie - me, Pravin Amre (centre) and Sachin Tendulkar after the Australia tour in 1992. Clicked at McDonald's in Singapore

Left: The Marathi folks of our team. With Kiran More (left) and Sachin Tendulkar (centre).

With South African cops. Loved the experience touring South Africa. It was a tough tour and even today it continues to be so for the Indian team.

No comment.

Had a lot of time for Ajay Jadeja and Manoj Prabhakar during my playing days. Pity how that panned out.

Top: I had many partnerships with Azhar, a very giving person. But I just could not warm up to him as a colleague. He was too different for me.

Above: Sydney, 1992. Onboard a roller coaster. Look at Sourav. He was terrified, while Sachin and I were laughing nervously in the back row.

from having seen the umpiring standards in international matches, I got even more frustrated. In that match, umpire Vinayak Kulkarni warned Abey Kuruvilla for running onto the danger area in his follow-through. I began to have a go at the umpire. I challenged his interpretation of the danger area.

Kulkarni held his ground. What infuriated me was the line of reasoning. While I quoted the law, he told me, 'I am the umpire, and this is my decision.' The umpires in domestic cricket looked like statues of authority to me, refusing to engage with the players. I was by now used to having a word with international umpires and reasoning things out.

Out of frustration I crossed the line. I began to mutter under my breath – but within Kulkarni's earshot – that he had no idea what he was doing out there. All my pent-up frustration – against all those umpires, all my wasted starts, all my run-outs, all those short balls – was now being directed at poor Kulkarni. He finally warned me that if I continued behaving like that, he would have to send me off the field.

I walked away, play resumed, but I was still fuming. I didn't think it would make a difference. 'Who cares about this silly Ranji game anyway?' I thought. So I told our wicketkeeper Sameer Dighe that I was going to have another go. Dighe panicked, and warned me, 'Don't do it, Sanjay, he will definitely send you off the field and report you.'

I stretched it until it snapped. I went up to Kulkarni and needled him again; he didn't waste a second and sent me off. Being sent off by the umpire should be the worst humiliation for a cricketer, a captain no less, but somehow I felt peaceful in the pavilion. I had unloaded all my toxins for the moment on poor Kulkarni.

This episode made headlines. I was officially reported to the BCCI. Jagmohan Dalmiya, always a players' man, let me off with a warning. The next time I met Kulkarni, I was back in the Test side, playing against New Zealand in his home town, Bangalore. He saw me and didn't know how to react. I went up to him, greeted him warmly, shook his hand, and had a chat. I ended up respecting him for doing the right thing. I deserved to be sent off the field. It was not right of me to behave like that just because I had played for India.

My frustration wasn't limited to umpires alone. As Mumbai captain, my team-mates too had to sometimes face the wrath of my misdirected anger. Once, on the field, I swore very badly at Sairaj Bahutule, one of the loveliest persons you could come across. I felt so bad later that I sought him out in his room. He was sitting with a few other junior players in the team, looking downcast. I apologized to him, unconditionally, in front of the juniors. I said I had no right to abuse him. Reprimand yes, but abusing is unforgivable.

Thankfully, this frustration never manifested itself in front of my family or friends, but it was clear that being denied a place in the Indian team was making me desperate. And my game was, as Bharatan wrote, going from one weakness to another. In the desperation to extend my career, now that the likes of Rahul Dravid and Sourav Ganguly were securing middle-order spots, I began opening the innings.

So I made one final comeback – as an opener against Allan Donald, Fanie de Villiers and Brian McMillan in 1996, despite the fact that by then their bowlers probably knew I could get slightly rattled by the short ball. Nevertheless, I still went ahead and opened against Donald, bowling at the peak of his career.

I got 34 in the first innings, and then got out just before lunch to Paul Adams, of all people. That infuriated me because despite my low confidence I had backed myself to open in a Test and had played the new ball and their best bowlers for two hours. I felt really confident this time facing a quick spell from Allan Donald. I kept telling myself to get on to the front foot, not worry about the short ball, because that way I would handle the short ball, my nemesis, really well and I did exactly so in that innings. I had confronted the short ball head on, opening the innings against the fastest, perhaps the most aggressive bowler in the world. It was like marching into a house on fire but I did it.

I survived Donald and the South African pace attack but got out to a rookie spinner. On 34 at the stroke of lunch.

That dismissal made me even more cynical – I began to tell myself that perhaps it was not meant to be. In the second innings, I got out to the short ball again. It proved to be my last Test innings. Caught fending.

That day, standing at the urinal next to me, Azhar made a telling statement – he had this way of nonchalantly saying something quite deep – 'Happens. When you start to age, it happens.' Azhar was thirty-three. He must have known. I was thirty-one. Azhar fought on. I couldn't. At thirty-three, I had already played my last Test for India.

*

What is batting, really? Is it scoring runs or scoring runs the right way? What is the right way? Who decides what is the right way?

When you are growing up, you don't think of these things. My game was completely natural. If I became a technically proficient player or a good player, it wasn't because I tried to become like anyone. The way I played was the way I played naturally, and people started saying I am technically good and all that. My strength was defence. I could never ever attack my way out of trouble.

I felt superior to a lot of batsmen around me because I felt comfortable in defence against good bowling on difficult pitches. When the team saw the green pitch in Sialkot, for example, I could see the blood drain from some of the faces. Me? I was happy because I knew now the team would know my worth a bit more. On this kind of surface only good defence works, and I had one. There weren't too many others, barring Tendulkar, of course.

I would feel pressure on flat pitches because I knew now that the more attacking flamboyant batsmen would come to the fore. I would feel my value was diminished. Even when out of form in Australia and in South Africa, it didn't bother me much that I was batting for two hours to get 30 runs. I enjoyed my time out there even if I was not scoring runs or hitting boundaries.

I guess it suited the team in those difficult conditions where I was playing off the hard new ball. Numbers 5 and 6 in Australia and South Africa are great numbers to bat at because the Kookaburra ball gets really soft and stops moving around after a while. I got first-hand experience of this when I suggested to coach Wadekar that captain Azhar bat higher in a chase at Wanderers. The idea was that Azhar was struggling, too, and I wanted him to have a go at the 318-run target on the final day. If it didn't work, I was confident I could save the Test. I ended up defending for three hours against the older ball for 32 runs without any trouble.

I never realized how long I was batting like that, defensively, on those pitches. It was like someone meditating and not realizing that an hour had suddenly passed. I was just proud of my defensive game. It was an era where people admired defensive players. When you left a swinging ball alone, the coach would applaud from behind the nets. As if you had hit a six. 'Well left' was a common compliment heard in nets and matches.

Even during the dark days of struggle, I could pull off a defensive innings. I scored that hundred against Zimbabwe after they racked up 456 in their first Test. Ian Chappell still ribs me about striking at under 25 per 100 balls against Zimbabwe, but I am proud of that innings because my team needed it to save the Test and avoid humiliation. Chappell even keeps naming the attack – Eddo Brandes, Mark Burmester, Malcolm Jarvis, Gary Crocker and John Traicos – to rub it in, but I don't budge. We agree to disagree.

Back in 1992, though, I will concede that Chappell did have a point. I was doing a radio interview after the day's play with Harsha Bhogle, and he waited for me to finish. After the interview Chappell grabbed me by the arm and said, 'Why aren't you pulling? Just pull one short ball from Merv Hughes, and watch the fun.'

'The problem is,' he went on, 'you are a good back-foot defensive player. You have to become more attacking.' Just imagine this legend waiting for a twenty-five-year-old upstart and giving him advice to overcome bowlers of his own country – that man stood for cricket. As I spoke to ABC that day, I overheard someone in the background prophetically say, 'We know what career he can have after he retires.'

Chappell knew that batting the right way without scoring enough runs was no good. Before Rahul Dravid played that breakaway innings – with V.V.S. Laxman – at Eden Gardens,

Chappell had made the same observation about him: He was paying far too much attention to defending well rather than scoring runs. Dravid was still better than me – at least he would get in position to pull the short ball and get the odd boundary. My 38 not out would be Dravid's 54 not out, and that completely changes the whole scenario. I had lost those shots to the short ball.

I just enjoyed batting defensively. It didn't bother me much what my score was after an hour, as long as I was playing flawlessly. I focused so much on playing correctly that sometimes I lost sight of what my real purpose at the crease was: to get runs. So if I scratched around while getting a score it did not please me. I am my harshest critic. Even in a double-century, if I played a couple of bad shots, I would think more about that. The next morning, people would be praising the double, but I would be thinking about those shots and practising to correct them.

I *had* to look good to all those who were watching me. Tendulkar, to an extent, was the same, but because of his prodigious talent he could not help but hit a good ball for a four every now and then. Unlike me, who would be stuck on 20 for almost two hours. This was the Mumbai school of batting. How you got your runs and against whom you got it mattered a lot. Just runs were not enough for Mumbai cricket.

One simple change that amazingly was never suggested to me by anyone during my struggle was to keep looking for singles while defending. I was content defending correctly instead of defending the ball in the gap and picking a single. On the contrary I would be so happy with a defensive shot that at times I wouldn't even notice that the ball has gone to the right or left of a fielder. I wouldn't even look for that single. If I had incorporated this aspect of batting at that time, I think my career would have turned out quite differently.

Instead, I went through a phase where I thought I should start hitting from ball one. But for that to happen, one needed a particular kind of bat swing. I could never do that. I tried it at a Challenger Series, a domestic one-day triangular tournament, and every time I tried to hit the ball in the air it got caught at midwicket. I got frustrated with my own game and its limitations.

I spoke to Dravid about this once. I told him, 'If I had to play a lofted shot – and for me it was a huge risk because I didn't have the game for it – I had to be absolutely right on top of the ball and play it to perfection for it to sail over the fielders. So I had to plan in advance.' Dravid agreed. He said, 'Yeah, for me also it used to be about planning to hit a big shot … that I would take a particular bowler on in the third ball of his over.'

I could feel my heart race whenever I decided that I was going to play the big shot the next ball because it was so against my nature.

I've seen Murali Vijay play like me sometimes, focused on playing correctly instead of trying to turn the strike over. Then, suddenly, in the next innings when he starts looking for some sharp singles, I tell myself that somebody gave him the right advice. Also, if he gets stuck on one score for too long, Vijay can just hit the ball out of the park.

My game wasn't like that, though, so picking up singles and rotating the strike was my only salvation, which I realized long after I had retired. Nor did I have a coach who could keep working on my game with me. We had the likes of Wadekar and Abbas Ali Baig as coaches. They were well-meaning former cricketers, but I never thought they were the kind I could talk to about what was going through my mind or what was going on with my batting.

At any rate, in those days we had just one coach – 'manager' is the more apt term – and one physio as support staff. A team coach has too many things on his plate to worry about one individual. Also, the approach of most coaches in those days was to be around the most successful player in the team when it was the man out of form that needed their attention the most. Players out of luck with their game were generally alone during our time, left to find their own solutions to their problems.

You did get good advice sometimes; Chandu Borde, for example, opened up my stance a little bit when he managed us on the tour of Pakistan. He found me getting too open when the ball was aimed at the middle stump. This was because I had become a little too rigid with my side-on stance. Not only did he open up my stance, Borde freed me up to explore the world on the leg side that I had forgotten in trying to play straight.

It was sheer luck that this even happened. Cricket was completely amateurish back then. That's where I respect Tendulkar. He thrived despite such an environment. Perhaps I needed a personal coach. Someone I could trust, someone who knew me well as a person, someone I could open up to. I admire young cricketers today who use the money they've earned from the IPL to employ personal coaches who can sort out some of the sensitive issues they go through, both technical and temperamental.

I remember this on the visit to South Africa in 1993. It was right towards the end of that tour where I hadn't scored many runs. An old man watched me bat from behind the nets. After the session, he came up to me and asked me to change my grip. He sounded like he knew what he was talking about. My grip was a typical Mumbai grip: the top hand on the bat handle is positioned in such a way that the V of the hand on the handle was in line with the outside edge of the bat.

This gentleman demonstrated how my arms could go no further than a certain height because of this grip. I was getting locked and could go no higher than a certain point to a rising delivery. He said that in South Africa you needed a grip where the V of the top hand is in line with the middle of the bat instead of the outside edge. He demonstrated it to me to show how easily my bat could go higher while defending a short ball if I had to.

Peter Kirsten saw me with this man, so later I asked him if he knew him. Kirsten said the guy knew his cricket so I could trust him. I never found out what his name was but it was a great tip. However, I didn't change my grip. It was a drastic change, I thought. It would have helped if I could discuss that piece of advice with a personal coach.

I wish I had the clear thinking of someone like Prabhakar. A bouncer is not that difficult a ball to negotiate if you think logically. It's the good-length ball that can get you out in more ways. When Prabhakar opened the innings, he would deliberately needle Devon Malcolm or Brian McMillan to bowl bouncers. 'If he bowls the bouncers, I can't get bowled or lbw,' he would say. They're bowled halfway down the pitch so one can see the ball a bit better. And at the Test level you can sometimes tell when someone is going to bowl a bouncer. When they run in, something changes in the last couple of strides, and you can almost predict there is a bouncer coming.

All you need is a clear mindset. When you hear stories of G.R. Viswanath and Virender Sehwag, you realize that their simplicity was a big reason for their success. For example, when an out-of-form Viswanath was advised by his well-wishers that he should stop playing the square cut because it had got him out early a few times, his response was, 'So where do I get my runs?' He stuck to playing his square cut, and came back to form. If the same advice had been given to me, I think I might have considered using it.

Sehwag, meanwhile, was intent on making the most of every ball bowled to him before one with his name on it came along. Matthew Hayden believed that batsmen were always way smarter than bowlers, so why worry about them too much?

True, it is a bit simplistic to think that way but I now feel it helps to be simplistic when you are playing. Thinkers by nature don't usually make good cricketers because a lot of cricket is about letting instincts take over. It pays not to ponder too much. All exceptional cricketers that I have got to know are people who didn't give their cricket excessive thought and brushed off their own failures. It is for this reason many of the greats of the game won't be able to give you much insight into the game.

There are exceptions, of course. Rahul Dravid is one. I spent a year with him in the Indian team. He used to dwell too much on every detail of his game, especially his failures and weaknesses. I worried for him then. He later told me that he developed a mental antenna of sorts, to warn him of the danger of overthinking. He knew his intensity as a player had the power to consume him. During India's tour of England in 2011, when he got three hundreds in the series when all others had failed, I joined him a couple of times for a quiet dinner. He made the effort to seek people out with whom he could spend an enjoyable evening with and take his mind off the game. We didn't talk cricket over those dinners.

As a commentator, I am older and more mature, so I have managed to keep this self-destructive side of me at bay. Also, as a player I had more weaknesses than I have as a commentator. Most importantly, though, commentary isn't as dear to me as playing cricket was. I don't obsess over it. It is just a job that I happen to enjoy.

I think if commentating meant as much to me as playing did, I would have self-destructed long ago. I have reserved that obsession for singing. Even when I am singing at home, it's the same. I make my wife, Madhavi, hear a little change I make sometimes while singing. Often, she sees no change, but I keep thinking about the important correction I've made from my earlier renditions. I keep hearing my recorded samples, and it's only rarely that I am happy with the outcome. I am a better singer now than I was ten years ago but I am less pleased with my singing now than I was then.

I recently cut a Rabindra Sangeet album in Kolkata. Madhavi was with me on that trip. This happened to be one of those rare instances when I was quite pleased with my performance – I'd recorded six Bengali songs in just three hours, and I liked the way I'd sung them too. I could see the surprise on her face when she saw me pleased with my own performance. It's something she is not accustomed to. Neither am I.

8

RETIREMENT

I DON'T REMEMBER the day after I retired as a first-class cricketer. I don't remember how I felt when I woke up on the morning after I had ended it all. The struggle, the torture, the frustration, the hopes, the camaraderie, the fame, the joy of being a Test and first-class cricketer had come to an end at the age of thirty-two. Rahul Dravid scored 5,925 Test runs after his 32nd birthday, Michael Hussey 4,638. Whereas I, with no real fitness issues, walked away from cricket in the year 1998, with no idea what I was going to do next. I did have the financial security of a job with Air India, but I knew I was not going to do a job just for money – I had to be passionate about it.

The memories of what preceded my last match are sketchy at best. This much I can be certain of: I wasn't sad. I had had enough. I was a Test discard. My last Test century had come five-and-a-half years ago. I had played only 15 Tests since that century against Zimbabwe. Fifteen Tests played across seven series, in which I averaged 28.09; each one played, in my mind at least, to save my career.

Now dropped from the India squad for close to two years, I knew making a comeback as an India batsman was never going to be easy. There were so many of them in good form, getting plenty of runs. You must do something more special than you did the first time around to convince selectors who have lost faith in you. During your first attempted comeback, the selectors do give you a chance to make it back to the team, but with every successive comeback attempt that interest wanes – the selectors prefer to move on.

As I'd mentioned earlier, the road to any comeback passes through Ranji Trophy and other forms of domestic cricket. To venture on to that road again was a scary thought. After playing ten years of international cricket, it was depressing to think of playing in front of empty stands day in and day out, in the hope that in one or two years I *might* just get another opportunity. Another opportunity to once again play to save my career.

I took great pride in being a public performer, a self-conscious one at that. I didn't want to look awkward while playing. Getting out fending used to bother me more than getting out for a low score. I used to think what will people say. 'What has become of this guy who was supposed to be the best Indian player against pace?'

The only thing worse was to have nobody discuss your game any more. Knowing that people were watching me play was a big high for me, and I'd get that only when I'd play at the highest level. The Wankhede Stadium used to get a few hundred – sometimes a thousand – spectators for Ranji Trophy games. They would be seated in the Garware Pavilion, right above our dressing rooms. So when you walked out to bat, you knew exactly how wanted and loved you were. I would always strain my ear to listen to the reception I got as I walked out, to hear the applause as they saw me coming out of the shadows, into the sun, and then in full view. After I'd been dropped during the home South Africa Tests in 1996 – during which I opened the innings in a desperate bid to stay in the side – I noticed I was not getting the same ovation as I used to get earlier. Was I not wanted as much any more? Maybe I imagined it, but I felt the crowd was not as excited to see me come out to bat as it was a few years back.

Without any hesitation, I decided it was time to pack up.

*

After that particular match, I called a press conference, announced I was going to retire after two more first-class games and came home to my sobbing wife, Madhavi. I had told her I was going to end it before I went for the press conference but when I came home it dawned on me that she too had been on the rollercoaster with me. When I returned, she hugged me and just broke down. Madhavi isn't generally a visibly emotional person. But that day, her reaction was purely because I think she felt sorry for me. She knew how badly I wanted the good times to come back, how hard I had tried. But that never happened and here I was, finally giving up the fight.

Even though I didn't discuss too much of my cricket with Madhavi, she had been witness to my frustrations over the last five years or so. I was exhausted trying to save my career, trying to swim against the tide, trying to stay afloat, waiting for the tide to turn so that I could at least enjoy being there. For almost four years, going into every game thinking it could be my last had finally taken its toll. Much later, I discussed that feeling with Rahul Dravid once. There were times in his tenure too when he had batted to save his career. He said it was a no-brainer: Playing to fulfil expectations was never as stressful as playing to save your career.

In those four years of struggle, I was frustrated I never got past that stage. This was an exasperation emanating from waiting for the big break that never came – I'd hoped it would be that one defining innings post the disastrous 1991-92 tour of Australia that would propel me back into the form and place I was in before.

I did have my share of moments full of false dawns and hopes. I scored a hundred against Zimbabwe at Harare in 1992 and scored some useful innings in ODIs, but a performance that would get my self-belief sky high never came. Every now and then I would get to a middling score and get exhausted and get out, only to earn me another chance and some more torture of playing to salvage my career.

Which is why, in 1996, I went to the extent of volunteering to open the innings with Nayan Mongia against South Africa in Ahmedabad. I scored 34 and 5, once again failing to build on a start. I was dropped from the playing eleven for the next Test, which we lost, and then from the squad altogether. That's when I first started thinking of retirement, although unlikely scenarios delayed it.

I spoke to Raju Kulkarni, Mumbai fast bowler who played three Tests for India. We'd grown up together and were quite close. He was honest in his response. He said it was not a bad decision. That a close confidant saw merit in my thoughts as opposed to doing the routine thing of motivating me to stay on made me look at it more seriously.

When I told Mumbai coach Balwinder Sandhu of my intentions, he said national selector Shivlal Yadav had told him they had taken note of my captaincy results with Mumbai, and were thinking of bringing me back, this time as India captain, at a time when India were going through a leadership crisis. Now that I look back, I know it would have been a highly controversial – nigh impossible – move but that air of expectation made me wait for a couple of India selections.

I used to also share my thoughts with Ravi Shastri, a senior I have a lot of respect for. At the time, he asked me not to retire because he had caught wind of Lalit Modi's idea of a big inter-city league – that was going to bring a financial windfall to players like me.

But I had already made up my mind – I was not going to change it for the lure of money. I never became a cricketer for the money; it was for the fame, remember?

Additionally, I could not stand the thought of keeping a youngster out when I wasn't enjoying playing Ranji Trophy cricket in the first place. First-class cricket can be quite depressing if you don't have an aim. Nobody cares, to be honest, and there's no atmosphere at the ground. Sachin Tendulkar, for example, enjoyed that life of being a cricketer, of just hitting balls, being with the team members, in the dressing room and things like that. I, however, could not imagine myself going through that grind.

During that time, Sourav Ganguly and Rahul Dravid made their debuts – both noteworthy – in England. I hoped against hope for a while but I just didn't have that will to keep playing. I used to enjoy my time, being with the players because there was less pressure playing Ranji Trophy. That also meant, in a twisted way, that I enjoyed it less. In my last Ranji Trophy game, against

Odisha, I just went out thinking I must get a hundred in my last appearance and I got it.

Once you've played a fair amount of international cricket as a batsman, you can get runs at the Ranji level quite comfortably. To me too, domestic cricket was not a challenge any more. If I, at the age of thirty-two, with my experience of playing international cricket, got hundreds in Ranji Trophy, who would care? Dominating at the lower level is something I found quite embarrassing.

It was out of sheer fatigue from swimming against the tide for four or five years – swimming, swimming, swimming, just to stay afloat – that I said 'enough is enough' and gave myself two matches to enjoy and bid farewell: against Odisha at Wankhede and against the travelling Australians at Brabourne Stadium.

*

The only aspect I enjoyed during this dark phase in my career after being dropped from the India team was captaining Mumbai. Time would fly when you focused on other people. It gave me a lot of satisfaction to help young players develop. I enjoyed that part of my job.

This was my second stint as captain, mind you. I am not proud of the first one, around 1991. I basically behaved like a spoilt, young international star among mere Ranji players. I was riding a wave of great self-confidence that came from my success at the international level. Even Tendulkar, and on occasion Dilip Vengsarkar, played under me. I bordered on the arrogant in the way I conducted myself that season.

Players who played under me tell me now that I was like a tyrant. I would throw tantrums and loved showing my displeasure towards a fellow team-mate's performance right in front of him and the rest of the team. That I was destroying their self-confidence in the process didn't strike me.

Sometimes it was an act. You can't be Mr Nice Guy all the time. Some players needed a little kick in the back side now and then, and they were certainly better for it after that. What I did to my good friend Raju Kulkarni once was certainly not a case of that.

The Mumbai team always had a fierce rivalry with Delhi. Our generation of players was consumed by it. I was no different. In a quarter-final game in the April heat of Delhi, we had secured a one-run first-innings lead to progress to the semi-final. We had then rubbed it in by scoring 719 runs in the second innings in 170.5 overs. I wasn't done yet. I wanted to inflict more damage. So, on an inconsequential final evening, when we had about 50 overs to bowl, I wanted my seamers to go out there, bowl fast and bounce their batsmen out of sight.

There was a general feeling then, largely fuelled by our seniors before us, that the Delhi boys didn't fancy fast bowling. I got my team together and told them of my intentions. Kulkarni, our lead fast bowler, senior to me in age and cricketing experience, protested and said it was a stupid idea. He suggested that we should take it easy and not exert ourselves too much because we had a semi-final to play in four days' time.

I looked at this as Kulkarni looking forward to a nice last session of putting his legs up and enjoying the DDCA hospitality. I blew my top when I heard that, and lashed out at him, telling him in no uncertain terms what I thought of that attitude. I told him if he was not on board with my plans he could jolly well stay inside, and that I was going to hold that against him.

I could see that the players froze seeing me lose it at a senior player. I thought Kulkarni deserved what he got. I even thought I'd sent a strong message to the rest of the team. I was told later that Naren Tamhane, former India keeper and the national selector at the time, an extremely likeable and sweet person, had entered the dressing room when I was in the act. Seeing me in that kind of mood, he quietly fled.

But I remember that day as the day Sachin Tendulkar won my heart. With Kulkarni not on the field, Tendulkar put his hand up and took it upon himself to intimidate the batsmen. This slip of a boy, just over five-feet tall, bowled six bouncers an over at times. He even hit Bantoo Singh, a Delhi top-order batsman, on the nose. There was blood all over the place. I remember feeling no remorse at the time.

In hindsight, it just feels so wrong, but this was a cocky twenty-five-year-old India cricket star at the top of his game. Nor is this kind of behaviour uncommon in sports. That is why I believe the captain of a team should never be the ultimate authority in a team hierarchy, and surely not of a state's or a nation's cricket.

The captain is too young to know what's best for the game. He is immature. He may know and have the skills to win matches, but doesn't always set the right examples. More importantly he doesn't have a long-term vision for the game. Players and captains aren't the people who should be deciding that. Take inputs from them for sure, but it has got to be older, more mature men to decide what's best for the game.

In my second stint as Mumbai captain, although I was also fighting for my India career, I used this behaviour of mine more judiciously. Now if I lost my cool, it was really an act, to motivate players, to pull them out of flux, all the while making sure I didn't demoralize them. We won the Ranji Trophy, beating Delhi in the first day–night first-class game in India, in Gwalior. We then went on to beat a strong Rest of India side, which included the likes of Navjot Sidhu, V.V.S. Laxman and Anil Kumble.

I would like to believe that I did a pretty good job captaining Mumbai during my second stint. I helped them win the titles but the greatest satisfaction I got was when I could make a difference to the life of young cricketers who had the same big dreams in their eyes which I too had once.

That's why I cherish the team meeting before my last Ranji match. Coach Sandhu gathered the whole Mumbai team in the Wankhede dressing room. Tendulkar was there too. They all spoke about how it was to play with me and what they felt the future held in store for me. It was quite amazing that Sandhu foresaw a future in commentary for me and the delicate issues that were likely to crop up. His benefit game was televised by TWI (Trans World International) and I had volunteered to commentate.

I remember Ballu-ji's words: 'Boys, Sanjay has now retired and in all likelihood will become a commentator, which means he will make public opinions about you, which will include criticism too. It's important that you accept that and look at a man who is only doing his job.'

How true Sandhu's words turned out to be. As a commentator, I went on to realize that if you played the game honestly and never shirked from a challenge, you did have a moral right to talk as an expert on the game even if you hadn't captained India or played in some 100-odd Test matches. That is why I never shy away from criticizing the greats of the game. I am sure they wonder how much cricket has Sanjay Manjrekar played himself to give him the right to criticize them, but I do it because it's my job to give my opinion on a public performer; that's what I get paid for. Anyone who refuses to do this is short-changing his employers and his audience. This is not a job where you make friends with your subject, but give the viewers and listeners your honest view of what's going on out there, and at the same time remain immune to what the player may think of you. You are not catering to him.

After Sandhu spoke, Amol Muzumdar made a speech and gave me a handwritten letter, which I read later. One by one, all the team members spoke. The more honest ones told me how frightened they were of my temper. I thought to myself, 'You guys are lucky, you should have seen me as captain in my first stint.'

All those boys were at an impressionable age as cricketers. I sensed that somewhere I had touched their lives quite significantly, and that came through in that gathering at the Wankhede dressing room. I felt pleased that I had made some impact on the lives of those wide-eyed young cricketers wanting to become big stars of the future.

Before my last first-class match, a week after that Wankhede game, I had an emotional moment with another senior cricketer, Ramakant Desai. He was the West Zone selector when I was dropped from the India side. I had just opened the innings despite my struggle against fast bowling and held my own in Ahmedabad, but I was dropped from the playing eleven for the next Test in Kolkata – this was the match where Mohammad Azharuddin hit Lance Klusener for five consecutive boundaries and scored the then-fastest century by an Indian. However, we lost that Test. Now heads had to roll, and I ended up paying the price even though I didn't play that Test. I was dropped altogether from the squad for the next Test.

I was angry. I told Tendulkar I was going to confront Desai about this. I asked Tendulkar to be there for the confrontation because he was the India captain at the time. Desai had acquired a reputation for being a bit of a pushover in that selection committee. I needed to be convinced he had put up a good fight for me.

Tendulkar found this awkward because confrontation was never his style. Impish that he was, he for some reason found it all very amusing. So, when I cornered Desai in the Eden Gardens dressing room, Tendulkar covered his face because he didn't want Desai to see him suppressing laughter. I asked Desai how he could have possibly dropped me. 'What were your reasons? How did you try to convince the others to retain me? Did you try to convince them at all?'

Poor Desai had no answer. This was not me being a bully but I was hoping I could have a dialogue with Desai and get some clarity because we felt quite close and friendly with him, despite the age gap.

Anyway, after one of my final games against the visiting Australians I found him standing just outside the dressing room of the CCI. I was playing for Mumbai.

He had stayed distant from me after my Eden Gardens confrontation, but seeing him there after so many days, my heart went out for him. I walked up to him and hugged him.

The poor man broke down into tears. He was shaking in my arms when I held him close. I am glad that I believe in forgiveness and moving on. I don't hold grudges against people. I just can't, even if I tried.

At the Ranji level there is more camaraderie among players. It's not as cut-throat as it is at the highest level. For some reason, I enjoyed playing state-level cricket more than Test matches at the highest level. We were more of a team while playing for Mumbai than for India. I might even have been wistful that night, but I knew I had two games left.

*

My last first-class match, thankfully, was more of a contest. Tendulkar was going to captain us in a tour match against a full-strength Australia side who were here for a Test series. Nowadays the hosts make sure the tourists don't get the best of practice by giving them ordinary sides to warm up against, but back then the gamesmanship was slightly different. We were looking to crush their confidence even before they started the Tests. And this was now a match big enough to be telecast live on TV.

After the Australians declared at 305 for 8, I came out to bat at No. 3 at 10 for 1. I joined Amit Pagnis, a pugnacious left-hand batsman, small of stature and quick of feet. He was a typical Mumbai product, a *khadoos* batsman. We both played out the Australian seamers, and now it was the turn of the pre-eminent spinner in world cricket, Shane Warne, to bowl his first over of that tour.

Warne had come to India with a big reputation. He was a mega star in world cricket, gracing the Indian shores after having bamboozled the world with his big leg-spinners. That series was going to be his first big test against the best players of spin, the India batsmen. The crowd at CCI, a few thousand, sensed the enormity of the occasion. I could hear a buzz around the ground when the ball was tossed to Warne.

Until now I had felt no real need to tell Pagnis anything apart from the usual words of encouragement in between overs. When I saw Warne get ready to bowl, my India-cricketer pride kicked in, and I walked over to Pagnis and told him to be a bit aggressive against Warne. 'Don't give him too much respect because of who he is,' I said.

Pagnis took my advice to heart so much that he just launched into Warne. Right from the first ball he faced, he began to hit Warne's stock leg-breaks through cover for fours. He didn't even bother keeping the ball down. He was only intent on hitting every ball that Warne bowled. When I had my chance against Warne, I, too, made sure that the tempo didn't diminish.

We were well and truly nipping the big threat for India in the bud there at the CCI. The variations that the world seemed challenged to tackle, were being easily spotted by our Mumbai batsmen, and the attack on Warne in that innings remained relentless. Pagnis scored 50 off 60 balls. I got 39 off 59. Tendulkar scored a double-century at more than a run a ball. At the end of that innings, the world's leading spinner's figures read 16-1-111-0 against a Ranji side. We went on to win the match by an innings, and things never got better for Warne on that tour. I would like to think Mumbai had a little hand in that by not allowing Warne to settle down.

The champion cricketer that Warne was, he was still in pretty good spirits even after being mauled by mostly domestic state-level batsmen. He didn't think of the experience as a big global star being humbled by some domestic cricketers. I will never forget that sight when he was walking back to the pavilion at the end of the innings, after all that punishment – he looked cheerful and had his arm around a young Mumbai batsman, chatting with him. It was Warne who was doing the listening.

It was evidence of a rare quality and Warne's great strength: When someone got the better of him, he did not think less of himself. He was happy to compliment the victor on the day. His lavish praise of Tendulkar and acceptance that he came second-best in a contest that the whole world was watching show how secure he was as a cricketer. Not once did he make an excuse for his failures on that trip to India. We must not forget that he was still recovering from a shoulder operation, and maybe because of that he wasn't quite at his best in that series.

I say this because I had played Warne at his best too, in the 1996 World Cup match at the Wankhede Stadium. When he bowled his leg-breaks in that game I saw a sight I had never seen before as a batsman. The ball came to me spinning viciously on its axis. I couldn't even see the seam; I saw just the leather. He used to impart tremendous side spin on the ball. I had to develop a new instinct where my bat had to come down at least a couple of inches wider to cover for the extra spin that he imparted on the ball. I didn't have to do this with any other spinner in my life.

Warne was a shadow of his former self in the CCI game. I still managed only a good start, and ran myself out, again, around the score of 40. As I walked back for what turned out to be the last time, having been run out for a middling score, it felt like a fitting conclusion. 'Sanjay, well done, you have made the right decision,' I told myself.

*

I don't even remember my first day after retirement. I must have woken up late I think – I hated waking up early but I had to do it since the age of twelve – so it felt nice, for a change, to sleep in. I don't remember much else.

There is no regret, nothing that I miss terribly from my playing days that makes me sad. Sure, there are a few things I miss, like travelling as a group, the banter, etc. But I don't miss the cricket.

I am proud the one quality in me that I know my wife, Madhavi, values a lot – because she is quite indecisive – is my clarity of thought and confidence in making decisions, especially the big, life-altering ones. There was no self-doubt, no confusion or uncertainty. I was absolutely sure that the time was right to hang up my boots. A tougher individual might have weathered the storm at the time I chose to retire, and might even have gone on to play 75 or 100 Tests, but I guess I wasn't such a person.

I believe big decisions have to be emotional decisions. Emotions dictate your state of mind, and the state of mind dictates your health, and nothing is more important in life than health.

Moreover, I could now go back to doing things that pleased me. Just the simple routines. Doing everything at a proper time. The clock rules my life. Dinner no later than 8.30 p.m., and not because I am hungry. When my mother was in hospital, days before she died, she did the same: She kept looking at the clock in that room to do her things, like she did all her life.

I never loved the game for the pure joy of hitting a ball. If cricket was not a popular sport in India, there was no chance I would have played it. It was my ticket to fame.

There were many individuals I'd come across who loved it much more than I did.

Ashish Parulekar, my close friend who broke his teeth when playing cricket in college, was one of those. Even now, whenever he gets the chance he plays cricket. He played club cricket for several years even when he was in his thirties, when he clearly didn't have any hopes of playing at a higher level.

Sourav Ganguly, for example, just loved batting. Tendulkar – he simply enjoyed hitting the ball, getting an upper hand over the bowler. I, however, didn't play for those reasons. I decided to get into commentary after retirement not only because it came naturally to me but also because it would keep me in the public eye. It's something all former cricketers want, even if we don't want to admit it.

It also takes care of the other need, especially for someone like me – I get to travel. I love being at home, but there's got to be travel before and after it.

Many retired cricketers fade into oblivion. Don't they miss the spotlight, or is it just me?

I don't miss playing at all. I never understood the logic of people turning up to see a faded player in action when you can see current players in their prime.

I didn't want to be one of those faded players in the spotlight. Whenever Ian Chappell runs into someone playing even after retirement, he asks, 'Why did you retire then?'

I was a bit like Chappell. I was happy not to touch the bat again. I have a cement pitch at my farmhouse where my son Siddharth often used to call me out to play. I wouldn't want to. I was quite happy sitting there and having a chat. I would prefer a quiet dinner, or just sit and have a stimulating conversation.

Cricket can be hard to get out of your system, though. A dear friend of mine, Somi Kohli, who makes Vampire cricket bats, used to make bats for me sometimes. At his factory, whenever he comes across a bat that he feels is just like the ones I used to play with, he promptly couriers it to me.

And I, retired for so many years now, keep telling him that I don't play any more. He says he can't help it when he sees a bat that reminds him of me.

Sometimes, when I pick up the bat and take my stance, it all comes back to me. I suddenly realize, 'Shit, this completes me.' It's amazing. When I take the stance, that position in which I spent hundreds of hours, the bat, I tell Madhavi, feels like an extension of my body that was missing, like an arm, and now I have found it. I feel complete – a whole person again.

I must have loved the game a little after all.

9
TEAM-MATES

WHILE I WAS with Mumbai and my Mumbai team-mates – the likes of Sachin Tendulkar, Vinod Kambli, Dilip Vengsarkar, Ravi Shastri and Sandeep Patil – cricket was this great team sport that was, above all else, fun. We were in it together, in victory and in defeat, in joy and in sorrow, in proud moments and forgettable ones.

When I debuted for Mumbai, in March 1985, we were a team that you couldn't beat easily. Haryana had Rajinder Goel and Sarkar Talwar, both prolific spinners in domestic cricket, so they'd prepared a turner because we didn't have a great spinner in our squad. When we travelled to Faridabad, I was not aware I was going to play. I had made it to the squad with six hundreds in a row in university cricket, and was now travelling for a knockout game. So Patil, the captain, saw me, a rookie, in the nets, thought I was in good form and wasted little time in deciding that I should play on that rank turner against Goel and Talwar.

We lost the toss, conceded a 28-run first-innings lead, losing all 10 wickets to Goel and Talwar, but came back to win outright. We just found a way. I scored 57 in the first innings, which until Patil made 59 in the chase was the highest score of the match and got me the award for being the 'best batsman of the match'. Kiran Mokashi, an unassuming off-spinner, registered his best figures, 6 for 66. As did Sandeep Patil, taking four wickets in the second innings, bowling slow seam and cutters off a short run.

Patil was a bit of an activist, with unique forms of protest. Our travel at the time used to be quite unorganized and haphazard. We'd travel by train a lot, which was okay, but often we would go unreserved. A Mumbai Ranji team, with India cricketers, would land up at Victoria Terminus (now Chhatrapati Shivaji Terminus) with reserved seats for only half of them. When that happened in one of my first matches, Patil got very upset. So, he said that in the next match we'd all play wearing black armbands, and we did. Mourning the death of our right to travel in a manner that befits a first-class side, I suppose. And back then, these things would become big news. Marathi journalists used to travel wherever Mumbai played. More journalists watched Ranji Trophy cricket in those days than they do today.

*

One of the most talked-about Ranji Trophy matches happened to be against Haryana, six years later. This was a final that attracted more emotion than some of the biggest international matches we have seen. There were Lalchand Rajput, Sandeep Patil, Dilip Vengsarkar, Sachin Tendulkar, Salil Ankola and me on one side and Kapil Dev, Chetan Sharma, Ajay Jadeja and Amarjit Kaypee on the other. We lost the toss, conceded 522, and had a 112-run first-innings lead, but came back to within three runs of the 355-run target in the fourth innings. We had only 190 minutes plus 20 mandatory overs to do it in.

Again, it was a game where Mumbai handed out a debut in a big final. I was the captain this time. I had seen Abey Kuruvilla in local cricket and played him in the nets. I looked at Tendulkar for confirmation. I had started trusting his judgement by now. I asked him, 'What do you think? He's quite good, no?' Tendulkar said yes, and we played him straightaway. Kuruvilla took four wickets in his first innings, and looked the part. He also was part of that 47-run last-wicket stand with Vengsarkar, which eventually ended in heartbreak.

This was a match where Kapil's experience came through. We were all playing with a lot of enthusiasm, but Kapil played smartly. A young Tendulkar's class stood out too. Although he didn't see us through, he scored 96 runs off 75 balls in a chase where some of the seniors of Mumbai cricket panicked. It was Tendulkar who started the counterattack, hitting five sixes, including a straight one off Kapil. Under pressure, he handled the situation extremely well, and I remember thinking that he was quite different from the rest.

As the match inched towards a close finish, and Vengsarkar played an innings for the ages, 139 off 139 balls, word spread and those who had left Wankhede dejected began to throng back. Tendulkar fell, and Vengsarkar began to cramp soon after reaching hundred. We still needed 114 when the mandatory overs began. On one leg, with Lalchand Rajput running his runs, Vengsarkar took matters in his own hands and hit three sixes and two fours in one over by Yogendra Bhandari.

I, of course, didn't watch any of it. Tendulkar had decided we were supposed to sit where we were sitting when he had begun the counterattack. So I – and Tendulkar – had to gauge what was happening from the noise from the stands. A loud cheer was a boundary. A boo was an appeal not given out. Silence meant a wicket. Between overs we would be told what was happening. All the finer details I gathered later.

Now that I think of it, this was very amateurish. As captain, I should have been watching the game closely and passing on any inputs to the batsmen but Tendulkar was adamant. Out in the middle, a seasoned veteran of international and domestic cricket along with a debutant No. 11 were trying to pull of an incredible win for Mumbai. With three required off 15 balls, though, there was a mix-up between Rajput and Kuruvilla. Vengsarkar stood stranded at square leg. He sobbed and wept as he walked back. It was a Ranji game but all of us, including international players, were deeply affected by it. It took some days for all of us to recover from it.

That game was played in much better spirit than the Duleep Trophy final in Jamshedpur four months earlier.

This was another first-class match that I will never forget.

There was Kapil Dev leading the North Zone, and Ravi Shastri leading us, the West Zone. This was a time when the cold war between the North and the West players came out in the open.

It was a contest between two quality sides with a liberal dose of international players in both. Both teams were desperate to prove their superiority over the other. Players on both sides were on the edge.

North Zone declared their first innings only after they had reached 729 for 9, having batted 223.1 overs.

They didn't want to leave us a window, never mind producing an outright result. I remember I got a hundred in what had become a first-innings shootout.

On 105, I played a forward-defensive shot off Maninder Singh. The ball went to Ajay Jadeja at silly point straight off the pad but my bat also hit the ground at the same time. Not surprisingly everybody went up in appeal – it was the thing to do then – and I was given out. The dismissal was moments before the tea break, so tea was announced by the umpires at the fall of my wicket.

Ravi Shastri, who had himself scored 152 in that innings, told me later that when he saw that I had not returned to the dressing room he asked others about my whereabouts. The players told him I had gone straight into the umpires' room. Shastri knew why I was there, so he came down to pacify me and get me away from them just in case I'd do something I would later regret. Well, that was the plan, but Ravi ended up joining me in having a go at the umpires.

Coming back to the match, North Zone took the first innings' lead and we went out to field again for not more than a session in what was a dead second innings.

But something happened in this mini-session that never happens in a high-profile first-class match. Rashid Patel from Baroda who played one Test for India attacked Raman Lamba with the stumps. Both sides had needled each other and it all had tipped over at the fag end of that five-day game.

The match was called off at that point thanks to the security personnel present to maintain order in the crowd trying to separate the two. Disciplinary action had to be taken. Madhavrao Scindia was the board president. Shastri and I, being the senior players, were called up for the hearing at Taj Palace hotel in Delhi.

In my statement to Mr Scindia and Mansur Ali Khan Pataudi, a special invitee in that committee, I said, 'Sir, we apologize for what happened. What he did was wrong and shocking to us too, but Indian cricket should be proud to see a first-class match being played with such intensity, passion and aggression.'

Both gentlemen had the ability to grasp what we as players were trying to convey and the matter was handled with great maturity. Lamba and Patel had to be disciplined, which they were, and we were let off with a warning.

This intensity we spoke of was something more than just a cricket rivalry, though. It was a deeper mistrust of each other when players from these zones played for India. It reminds me of the advice Sandeep Patil gave me a day before my Ranji debut. He asked me in the team meeting what number I would want to bat at, and I said – as you expect a youngster to say – whatever was assigned to me. He told me to never say that in the India team; otherwise they will keep sending me anywhere they want. 'When you are in the India team they will make you a scapegoat and bat you at any number that suits them,' Patil advised. 'Always let them know where you want to bat.'

As far as advice goes, here is a funny one, from Raju Kulkarni before my Ranji debut. He shared it with me more as a friend than as a senior. He said that if I wanted to get into the groove for a big game I should start polishing my shoes the night before. Back then we had boots that we used to polish. 'Just clean your shoes, apply polish, leave them to dry, it'll get you into the groove.' I listened to him like a young obedient cricketer would. We had a big laugh about it a few years later.

The tables turned on me somewhat when it was my turn to give advice. To a fourteen-year-old Tendulkar. This was at the time when he was about to make his Ranji debut. At the Wankhede Stadium the next day I was around, but not playing, so I took him aside and told him: 'Tomorrow you'll be making your debut, but this is Ranji cricket so it's no big deal. Test cricket, yes, maybe there is something there, but this is only slightly better than the school cricket you have played.' Although my advice was definitely less bizarre than Kulkarni's, Tendulkar pulled my leg later about how patronizing I was as a senior.

I was so lucky to have players like Kiran Mokashi around in the Ranji team. He was a big supporter of me and Tendulkar from our very early days. He was the kind of character who was in the team more to help others, and he wanted to make them better players in any way he could.

Often, after our Mumbai net sessions got over he would tell me or Sachin, 'Come, I'll give you more practice.' And he would be the lone bowler doing overtime just to make us better players.

Those were the innocent days. The Ranji days. This was when team-mates played together to win, and help make each other better cricketers.

*

Things were different at the international level, I soon found out. Everybody lived in their own bubble, looking after their own interests. I played for India at a time when the dressing-room atmosphere was not enjoyable at all. What I disliked most was the excessive respect that the seniors expected.

The seniors from the north were all addressed as 'paaji'. They didn't prefer anything else and they liked it too – that people got up every time they walked in. This didn't help team-building at all.

It was because of such things that the gap between us youngsters and the seniors was too large – it didn't even feel like a team since no one could speak or behave freely.

If anyone without a clue about cricket would have walked into the Indian team meeting, they would have easily known the hierarchy – the senior players, the superstars and the juniors.

For a typical team meeting, we would all assemble in one hotel room, usually the team manager's. We didn't have a special conference room or a team room, like they have now. We would all cramp into that one room, wherever we could find space. The seniors sat in the chairs and the sofa, some sprawled on the bed or the sofa while the juniors sat upright on the floor.

Meetings were generally scratching the surface on tactics and strategy. The approach was never thorough.

Often they would end in five minutes. Kiran More would leave the room angry. 'Is that it? Is that our team meeting? Is this how we are going to win tomorrow?' he would ask as he'd walk back to his room. More was not one of those big star players in the team, but was ready to give everything for Indian cricket. He would always get bumped up the order if the second new ball was taken while the bigger names went down a number. I had a lot of time for More. He was a real fighter.

These meetings, therefore, were more a formality. Even though we spoke Hindi on the field – Punjabi and Marathi were the other dominant languages off the field – our team meetings, for some reason, would be conducted in English.

I found Mohammad Azharuddin's team talks as captain quite funny. They were mumbling monologues. They sounded exactly like the old short-wave radio transistors. Like the sound waves on the radio, the volume of his voice would also go up and down.

Those of us sitting away from him would try to catch and make sense of whatever we could hear.

Sometimes we would exchange glances and even suppress a laugh when his voice went really low, and we couldn't hear a thing. We'd see his lips moving though.

Kapil would sometimes take it upon himself to round up the team meeting, and he would go, 'Right, guys, as we have decided, Mannu is the old ball, and I am the new ball.'

Of course, we all knew what Kapil meant by this. We had all become experts at understanding his English. He spoke English like a reporter's notes: just the operative bits. We knew Kapil meant to say that Manoj Prabhakar would bowl fewer overs with the new ball because he was proficient with the old ball.

The Kapil I now work with in the commentary boxes is a completely different person compared to the team-mate he was. The present Kapil is the real deal: a sweet, humble and amiable man. Kapil the player was nothing like that. He was caught up in the Indian cricket climate, I guess, where the legends and the superstars almost felt obliged to behave in a certain manner, especially in front of juniors and newcomers.

I could understand the need for the iconic players to maintain that image in public, but they didn't behave too differently in the dressing room and in the nets.

On the 1989 tour of the West Indies, Vengsarkar was the captain. This was the tour just before which Vengsarkar had brought in a Mumbai schoolboy, Tendulkar, to the India nets and made Kapil bowl to him. Now another Mumbai batsman, me, was in the first eleven.

I didn't get to bat in the rain-affected Guyana Test, but will never forget the nets before the Barbados Test. Kapil would hardly ever bowl in the nets a day before the Test but when I came in to bat, not only did he bowl, he made it a point to bounce me. I don't know what the reason for that could have been. I remember being taken aback but I played him well. Then he would applaud and say, 'Yes, that's the way to play. Well done!' It was the only time he bowled to me like that in the nets.

In the Barbados Test in that series, I went on to get a hundred, but I did so with the help of the tail. I was in my 70s when No. 9 Arshad Ayub joined me. He was also my room-mate and we had developed a nice rapport. He was happy that I was still batting and that I could finally clinch my place if I got to a hundred. '*Chhodna nahi,* don't give it up,' were the first words he spoke when he came out to the middle. He batted for close to two hours with me and saw me through to my first Test century. That was a real humbling moment, Arshad Ayub at the Test level doing what Mokashi did at the Ranji level, but all too rare at the India level.

There was just too much 'respect' and leeway given to seniors. Never did the same yardstick apply to all players.

I used to ask Ian Chappell whether it was the same in his Australian team.

He would tell me that he had to actually cop more banter than the rest because he was captain. That was the Australian culture. They respected their captain but could also tease him. Nowadays when I see all these youngsters knock a captain on the head I find it odd but nice. It was different in our time.

Only towards the end of my career, under Ajit Wadekar, did things change a little. He brought a certain seriousness to team meetings. When he first joined, he silently watched for a couple of days what was going on, and then on the third day he categorically told Kapil that he'd have to bowl to at least three batsmen in the nets. At this stage of his career Kapil hardly bowled in the nets, he batted and bowled when he felt like. Like most seniors at the time. I could see Kapil was taken aback when he was told this.

At the start of my India career it was easy to see that there were two teams within the team: a North Zone team and a West Zone team. Players from the North Zone team of India wouldn't speak freely in the presence of a member from the West Zone team of India. It was quite terrible. What's more, they were always suspicious of each other, and never warmed up to each other. This began to change only towards the end of my career. Ajay Jadeja was one player who began to break down this North–West divide. Jadeja was a fun-loving guy. He came from Delhi, he was almost like an adopted son of Kapil, who adored him. But Ajay also became very friendly with the Mumbai boys who were closer to his age. And then came Javagal Srinath, who was big on team unity. As the number of players from the south grew – Srinath, Prasad, Kumble – the tension between the North and the West players started to recede.

Nevertheless, the early nineties was a bad time to be in the India team – there was just too much mistrust, envy and hatred among senior players. I remember when Kris Srikkanth was made the captain in Sharjah, one senior remarked, 'Look, a constable has been made the commissioner.' What chance did Srikkanth have as captain?

When we had a different captain few months later, yet another senior said to me, 'Good we lost the match. This captain won't last too long now.' So it was a horrible time to be a part of the India team, and it showed in our performances too, especially overseas and against Pakistan who were led by a senior who had his heart in the right place.

In many ways it was a time when seniors were insecure – it was about looking out for yourself as there wasn't much hope for the team to perform well. Indian cricket was diseased during this time. Players avoided tough situations and oppositions.

They returned fit to play against weaker sides at home. What was worse was that these very players actually managed to get away with this approach and ended up having longer careers and better cricketing statistics than those who didn't shy away.

I remember an episode from our tour of Pakistan. I found myself batting with someone who refused to take a single and face Wasim Akram, clearly the quickest and most dangerous bowler in that side. This went on for almost an hour. I was stuck at one end facing Wasim while my partner ensured that he was doing nothing of the kind that would fetch him a single at his end and bring him on strike to face Wasim.

Out of frustration, I complained through a substitute who came to us at some point. I was hoping the captain would send a message to my partner so that he would rotate the strike.

Believe it or not, I got a message back requesting me to let it be and continue focusing on my batting. This was a typical Indian cop out of those days. If Imran Khan was leading such a team, this batsman would never have played for his country again. However, that was an era when such players flourished and that batsman was smarter than me to know this.

Ravi Shastri, Sandeep Patil, Sunil Gavaskar would all tell us stories about all those India players who would go missing when West Indies visited India. Back in Mumbai, former players like Dilip Sardesai would identify such players from his era, telling us all about the *phattoo* (scared) players in his team. Some of them would be in senior administrative roles, as selectors, aged over sixty, but even then Sardesai would not spare them. 'Look at him, he is a selector now, but he was such a *phattoo* player.' At an impressionable age, these stories were drilled into our heads. We weren't going to be one of those *phattoo* players ever.

In complete contrast to my batting partner in Pakistan was Manoj Prabhakar. In 1994-95, when I was making my comeback to Test cricket, I was struggling in the dying moments of a day's play in Mohali. This was the Test in which we were bowled out for 114 in the second innings, but in the first innings we'd scored 387. I had scored two fifties in my first Test on comeback, but again had a couple of low scores in Nagpur. My confidence was a bit shaky, and I desperately wanted to make it to the end of the second day after West Indies had scored 443 and had removed Sidhu for a duck.

Kenny Benjamin, who had troubled me throughout the series, was at it again.

The other strike bowler was Courtney Walsh, but it was Benjamin who had the wood on me in that series. He bowled short of a length, and got the ball to seam both ways off the pitch. Throughout the series I had failed to pick him either from his wrist position or from the seam in the air.

So I did something a bit outside my Mumbai batting character. I went up to Prabhakar, told him of my problems with Benjamin, and asked him if he could take more of him till stumps. Prabhakar immediately responded, 'Arre … you should have told me earlier in the series. I would not have let you face him at all.'

Prabhakar went on to score a hundred the next morning. Once again he had found himself opening the batting since the West Indies were in town. This is why I had a problem with the Indian cricket culture at the time: players like Prabhakar were not respected by the captain and the seniors; their value was never properly appreciated. To some extent that contributed to their being frustrated and becoming bitter and negative about Indian cricket. Across the border, Prabhakar was exactly the kind of player who'd have flourished under the captaincy of Imran.

At the 1992 World Cup, there was this legendary photo of all the players on a ship. Since I was an Imran fan, I went up to chat and get a photograph taken. We caught up; he wanted to be updated on our recent cricket; he kept track of my performance. During that chat, Imran was full of praise for Prabhakar; he said Prabhakar put in a better all-round performance than Kapil on that Australian tour. Prabhakar was an Imran kinda player. He was a bit different from most Indian cricketers at the time. There were just a handful like him during my time, especially my early days in the India team.

He was selfless, opened the batting as well as the bowling in Test cricket. I don't know how many people would do that, even in modern-day cricket. It's a rare feat not just in Indian cricket but also at the international level.

He was a street fighter to the core. The Pakistan team under Imran was filled with such players; it was Pakistan's best ever team.

Prabhakar played like a rebel in our team, and this was the source of his performance and output. He overachieved, if you ask me. He wasn't that gifted.

My theory is that he never forgave Kapil for what happened on the 1986 tour of England. He was a part of the original squad; Chetan Sharma got injured, but Kapil called up Madan Lal from the leagues to replace him for the Headingley Test, leaving Prabhakar out and forever angry.

Not many know this, but Prabhakar was the first in the India team to learn and develop the art of reverse swing. He, in fact, educated Kapil about it. Kapil was quite a purist that way with his bowling.

Despite all his suspicions and criticism of the system, Prabhakar was happy to share whatever he learnt with anyone.

I once shared a room with Prabhakar in Sharjah. You get to know a person really well when you share a room with him over a couple of weeks, and he turned out to be a decent person.

We both had a good tournament as roomies and he wanted to continue that arrangement in 1992 in Australia. I had, however, already committed to sharing rooms with my friend and the sweetest person you will ever meet, Venkatapathy Raju.

I am not a superstitious person, but I remember thinking, would the Australian tour have turned out differently had I shared my room with Prabhakar?

I remember he once took me aside in Delhi during a match. By that time, my relationship with him was strained. I was angry with him when he pretended to be injured in one county game in England in which I was supposed to rest. Because he opted out, I had to play. And I held that against him.

It was to set that right that he had taken me aside to have a chat. He said, 'C'mon Sanjay, we are going to be playing together for a while now; both of us are important players in this side. People take advantage of such things and make sure we become even more distant from each other. So let's bury the hatchet and get on with it.'

My answer was an instant yes. His approach to resolving our relationship was extremely rare in Indian cricket. No many were known to have such upfront chats and take action. Generally, no one wants to be confrontational; they'd rather do everything on the sly.

But Prabhakar was a man full of surprises. After all, I was one of his victims in those secret recordings for *Tehelka*.

I'm still amazed at how it all unfolded. I was invited by Chandrakant Pandit, former India keeper and batsman and a dear friend, to speak to his students to inaugurate his cricket academy at Andheri in Mumbai. When I reached the venue, Pandit told me that Prabhakar was also coming. I found it strange, but Pandit said he was in town, so he invited him too, and Prabhakar had immediately agreed.

The moment our work was done at the academy, Prabhakar hopped into my car, saying he wanted a lift till Juhu. I was driving and he sat in the front, next to me. I told him to leave his handbag – it seemed like a gym bag – in the back seat but he insisted on carrying it on his lap. Somewhere along the way, he steered our conversation towards match-fixing, especially about matches in Sharjah. One match in particular – the one we'd lost in fading light.

Now, I was not naive. I had a lot of respect for Prabhakar as a cricketer and admired some of his qualities as a person, but he was never in my inner circle of friends because for some reason I could not fully trust him. So I gave him nothing. He persisted with his probing questions, but I remained guarded. Maybe with Kiran More and Sachin I'd have been more forthcoming but with him I wasn't.

Also, with respect to the Sharjah game we were talking about, I still believe if Sachin and me had hung around longer we would have won the match.

Despite all my admiration for him, it was due to that conversation in the car that day, and how it was recorded under the garb of a sting operation, that Prabhakar failed the most important test for me: the test of integrity. We became distant again. I met him after many years, in 2016 during the World T20 when he was coaching Afghanistan. I could not help but greet him warmly.

Time heals old wounds, I guess.

*

It was under Azharuddin's captaincy that the lines between West and North Zone's players started to blur. By this time, Sachin had become a big force within the team and he was not in anyone's camp. That certainly helped in bridging the divide.

By nature, Azhar was not a leader. Leadership was thrust on him and he did the best he could. But I think leadership did change him. For some reason, he spent more time with people other than his own team-mates. I wonder if that was deliberate.

When I became Mumbai captain, I remember being advised by my senior colleague in the team: 'Don't hang around with the younger players too much. A captain needs to keep his distance and maintain a certain dignity.' At the time – and even now – I thought it was a stupid piece of advice. Fortunately, Virat Kohli does not believe in this 'senior–junior' culture too much.

I'd like to think that was an important reason why Azhar was not an inspirational leader that the team would give their right arm for. We just didn't know him too well, what he was all about.

As captain, he was generally not animated on the field. If you messed up during play, you would not know if he was upset. But he would rant about it in team meetings.

'Why don't you tell them there itself?' An anguished voice of Manoj Prabhakar had once responded to Azhar's rant. He was right. Why not nip it in the bud instead of waiting for the damage to be done and then reprimand?

As a tactician, Azhar wasn't great. The main feature of his captaincy was to leave things to the Almighty. He had great faith in destiny, and somehow on good days he felt India was destined to win, that someone up there was conspiring to get him to lead India to victory. That's why he wouldn't tamper too much with what was happening out there, and would do just the basic, textbook stuff with regard to bowling changes and field placements.

In hindsight, it seems as if there was indeed a touch of amazing destiny in how everything worked out for Azhar. In the first Test on the 1989 tour of Pakistan, he was out of form and was set to be dropped from the playing eleven. Raman Lamba was supposed to replace him, but Lamba injured his toe in the nets. Azhar, therefore, had to be played, and while he didn't turn it around with the bat, he loved fielding and took five catches in the first innings.

It was a big game for both sides and we ended up securing a draw thanks in part to his fielding. He couldn't be dropped now, so he played the next match, got runs and secured his place in the team. One year later, Raj Singh Dungarpur, then president of the BCCI, asked him, '*Mian, kaptaan banoge*?'

As captain, when the opposition seemed to be getting away with the game, Azhar would sometimes get all of us together during the drinks break, not to give us a pep talk to lift us but to seek advice. Everybody would give their inputs, and based on it Azhar would sum it up saying, 'Okay, so I will bowl Raju for three overs from this end, Mannu three overs from that end, and Kapil Paaji and Sri after that.'

He would then go take his fielding position, relieved that the next seventy-five minutes were sorted. It meant he need not think about captaincy for a while. He could now concentrate on what he enjoyed, his fielding.

This approach was responsible for some out-of-the-box and brilliantly successful moves Indian cricket witnessed – like Tendulkar bowling the last over against South Africa to win the Hero Cup semi-final in 1993. He was happy to go along with other people's advice; he did not have an ego in such matters. Perhaps he was smart in knowing his limitations, something that takes a lifetime for the not-so-smart to realize.

The 1992 World Cup game against Pakistan in Sydney is another example where Azhar listened to our suggestions. I remember Pakistan had lost two early wickets, one each to Kapil and Prabhakar in their first spells. Then Aamer Sohail and Javed Miandad had a partnership, which was important to break. Once Tendulkar did that, we pleaded to Azhar to get Prabhakar back on for a couple of overs. We knew the new man Saleem Malik was the big wicket, and as per his protocol Azhar would have got Prabhakar back on much later. Azhar gave in to our demands, and Prabhakar came on to remove Malik, and India went on to win another game under Azhar.

This belief that Azhar had, that an angel was watching over him, was quite incredible. Towards the end of 1995, Azhar's stock as player and captain was plummeting, and Tendulkar was bigger than he had ever been before. The clamour for Tendulkar to become captain was getting louder with each passing day. India wanted a change; the selectors could sense it, and so did Azhar.

This tournament later went on to be known as just Challenger Trophy, but back then it was called Challenger Trophy One-day Selection Tournament. The name made the purpose of the tournament obvious. India, India A and India B played in the triangular, and this was the stage to stake claims for selection.

Azhar knew, and we all knew, that it all came down to the final of this tournament. He had seen enough of Indian cricket not to know it. Azhar was captaining India, while Tendulkar India A. If Tendulkar could lead his team full of youngsters – promising ones, mind you, like Rahul Dravid, Sourav Ganguly – to win against an almost full-strength India side, it would be convenient for the selectors to make this big change.

This tournament was played on a poor pitch in Hyderabad where every game was low-scoring, and the chasing side never won. You knew you had to win the toss and bat first to win the match. So out walked Azhar, on the last day of the year 1995, knowing his fate as captain depended on the toss. We all looked out to see what was going to happen, some concerned about the match, but some others knowing fully well how massive that toss was for the future of Indian cricket.

Azhar, of course, won the toss. When he came back, I told him, 'Well done, Azzu.' He looked at me, smiled a knowing smile and said, 'I knew I was going to win it.' The expression on his face when he said that conveyed so much to me. It had all come down to this one outcome, an outcome beyond his control, and he knew that invisible power, the guardian angel, would take care of him again. It indeed took very good care of him as we went on to beat India A by 33 runs, and Azhar went on to captain India in the 1996 World Cup.

I witnessed first-hand this divine power come to his rescue when he got that sensational hundred against South Africa at Eden Gardens, the joint-fastest Test century by an Indian. Azhar had had that captaincy lifeline, but after the World Cup semi-final loss, he lost his captaincy and went through a horror run with the bat. His self-confidence had hit rock bottom. He was hit on the arm earlier in the game. While the X-ray did not reveal any damage, he was not very keen to bat at his No. 4 position. Madan Lal, the manager at that time, didn't buy it, and insisted that Azhar was not going to bat down the order.

Against his will, Azhar went out to bat against a strong South African attack, and scored one of his best Test hundreds. In celebrating his century, he gestured angrily towards the dressing room, presumably at the manager, who had questioned his courage. I was not playing the game, so I took a drink to him in the dressing room after the innings. He had just come in, and taken his pads off. I knew how much that innings meant to him and how crucial it was for him to keep his career afloat. I looked into his eyes, and said, 'Well played, Azzu, *chabook*.' *Chabook* was the Mumbai cricket term for brilliant.

He looked at me humbly and said, 'I just threw my bat around,' – then his head pointed upwards – 'He took care of the rest.' It was an honest confession made at a very tender moment. I felt very happy for him.

Of course, I would like to think all this was possible only because he had the skills to do it. And yes, his attacking approach towards batting. When down in the dumps, I believe a defensive player needs a little more luck than an attacking player. That's because an attacking player needs less time to get out of troubled waters than a defensive one.

Today, I don't know what to make of Azhar. There are obvious suspicions of match-fixing that follow him, but there was another side to Azhar that I had seen.

Thrust into captaincy more to break the cliques in the team that were causing some trouble to the administration in the late '80s with pay hikes, etc., Azhar was a generous and unassuming man. On his first tour as captain, to New Zealand in 1989-90, he and his team had to deal with the worst team management that could be assembled. It derived some perverse joy out of bullying young cricketers.

We had a young Tamil Nadu off-spinner called M. Venkataramana who didn't have a good outing in one of the side games. In the team meeting that followed, he was asked by the coach, 'Tell me, why did you bowl so badly?' How does one answer such a question? Poor Venkat remained silent. 'Cat got your tongue?' the coach screamed. 'Speak up.'

I could not believe my eyes when Venkat was asked to stand like a kid in a classroom. That night, the team management had a lot of fun at our expense.

After the ordeal was over, we dragged ourselves to our respective rooms. Tendulkar and I were room-mates on that trip. After about five minutes, we heard a knock at our door. It was Azhar at the door. He entered the room, and gave us a warm hug, and asked us not to take it to heart. We felt much better after that, knowing that our captain was in it with us and was like a big brother to us.

Azhar is also the most charitable person I have known in cricket. The Mafatlal Group of companies, who used to employ quite a few cricketers, once organized a function at the Taj Hotel in Mumbai as part of a little incentive scheme for Indian cricketers. There used to be cash awards for the outstanding performers, which were to be presented at this function. Amol Muzumdar was due to win a prize for his exceptional performance at the first-class level; so he was there along with us, the India team.

Muzumdar told me that after the function got over, Azhar had shook hands with him and congratulated him on his performance, and then put his finger on Muzumdar's lips and whispered, 'Don't tell anyone.' While shaking Muzumdar's hand, Azhar had slipped in a roll of bank notes, all the cash that he had won at the function. (Yes, they gave out cash prizes, not cheques, at the ceremony.)

I have seen cricketers do charity but it is mostly by playing benefit matches for a cause, giving their personal items to be auctioned or being present at events to raise money. To take out money from your own pocket and give it away is real charity. Very few can do that. Azhar could.

Earning is one skill, spending on others is completely another; there are not many I know who possess both.

The Azhar story is quite the story, isn't it?

*

I didn't time my Test career right, and had I played longer I would have enjoyed the better phase of Indian cricket that came after I retired. My big regret will always be that I never got to play for a strong India side in a happy, healthy team atmosphere. I told Tendulkar in 2003 in South Africa during the World Cup that it was good seeing him a part of this, the happy chapter of Indian cricket along with what we saw together in the '90s. My career was only about one chapter. It is no surprise that out of the 37 Tests I played, we won just seven and lost 13. There were 33 wins and 38 losses in the ODIs I played.

As for me, batting during my first three years, I played for survival. At the highest level, I played mostly outside India – only 10 of my 37 Tests were at home. My memory of Test cricket is of being at the receiving end – being in the outfield for three days and batting twice on consecutive days.

In 1989, I went to the West Indies, then Pakistan, and after one Test versus Sri Lanka it was time to tour again. So my memory of playing Test cricket was always of being in a position inferior to the opposition.

Nowadays, it is so good to see fans getting disappointed when India lose overseas. It shows that there are expectations. Back then even we weren't expected to compete. I don't think any of us had entertained any serious hope of beating Australia when we went down under or beating the West Indies on their own turf – it was always about leaving your own individual mark. Winning was out of the question. Even when we went to New Zealand, there was no hope of winning. So there was no question of going to a team meeting and actually planning how we were going to win. Plans follow hope – if there is no hope, there are no plans.

Perhaps the India seniors just felt inferior to the opposition, and it trickled down from there. It was different in ODIs where we had won the World Cup and the World Series in Australia, a format that allows lesser teams to compete. But in Test cricket success came the hard way. And it happened only in little sparks. I largely played during the period after Gavaskar had retired, and Kapil was not getting any better.

For us, when it came to winning matches, if it happened, it happened. Nobody *really* believed we were good enough to win. I once saw an India captain giving an interview to a TV channel after getting a hundred. He looked thrilled as he answered questions about his hundred with a beaming face. It didn't bother him one bit that his team had lost the Test.

Then – I believe out of sheer accident – Dravid and Ganguly joined Tendulkar as world-class batsmen. Along the way arrived V.V.S. Laxman and Virender Sehwag. For the first time since my debut, India had a batting line-up that could get runs and dominate in overseas conditions too. They could all play shots on quick, bouncy pitches. That was one clear difference between the earlier teams and this team. I don't think Indian cricket trained them to be such players. They just grew up wanting to be good players of pace and bounce. Suddenly, India didn't have a sitting-duck opener in foreign conditions, and they had four world-class batsmen out of six. In my time – and I was part of that problem – most of the time it was Tendulkar alone.

And as these new boys started to taste success, the attitude of the Indian fan too changed. In our time the fans demanded very little. They worshipped cricket blindly, and were star-struck by cricketers. It was amazing that when we would be in the dressing room, the fans would be looking at us and not at the game. Those close to the dressing rooms didn't take their eyes off us for the whole game.

I got a taste of this star-struck nature of cricket fans when I came back from Australia in 1992. I was a star when I arrived in India and I was getting mobbed whenever I went shopping in Mumbai. I was surprised – I was a big flop on that tour, so why the fanfare? After some thought it became clear: It was the Channel 9 TV coverage of the games!

We looked like proper cricket stars in those coloured outfits in the backdrop of Australian grounds with Channel 9 commentary. Fans also got to see what we looked like. This was vastly different from the 1989 Pakistan series coverage, which offered only a conventional two-camera view of the action. I was the success story of that Pakistan tour. People had heard of me but they didn't know what I looked like.

No wonder then, after that four-and-half-month dismal tour of Australia, we were thronged by fans on our arrival at Mumbai airport. They were there to see the people in flesh, the same players they had seen on TV for four months.

10
COMMENTARY

AS A PLAYER, I had an opinion about everything. I was not afraid of sharing my opinion in team meetings. By nature, I am extremely judgemental. All these turned out to be the very qualities I needed in my life post retirement: as a commentator. Getting into commentary was a seamless transition. Right from my first game as a commentator, I felt at home. Except that watching the game so closely on the monitor was a new thing for me. I remember thinking every leg-before appeal was out, but by the second game I was all right.

I was not educated in the best English school in Mumbai, but the language was not a big hurdle in my new profession. My school was good at basics. It made our grammar sound. Diction and fluency came later. My sisters studied in a convent school, and had good command over English. This would become evident when they fought. English might as well have been their official fighting language – they would switch from Marathi whenever things heated up.

They would constantly pick on my English, especially my pronunciation. When they came to my school's annual functions, they'd find faults with my teachers' English as well. It's thanks to them that my English didn't turn out like my teachers'.

I have always had a flair for languages, and I loved English as a subject, so I learnt fast. Even if I could not speak as evocatively as, say, Harsha Bhogle, I could articulate my cricketing thoughts quite easily. Language was never a constraint in speaking my mind. Even today, I like to use language for its main function: to express, not to impress.

I could see that people were generally impressed with my work in my early days as a commentator. There hadn't been many iconic Indian commentators; expectations therefore weren't too high.

Once I started doing this job regularly, I realized it could be a long-term professional option for me.

Naturally I wanted to get better at it, and not restrict myself to expert analysis, which is what's expected of former cricketers. When you start off, you are put in the role of a 'colour' commentator alongside a more seasoned commentator who handles the descriptive part of the coverage. The lead commentator is more the spine of commentary while the colour commentator can afford to take a back seat and talk only over slow-motion replays or analyse the play and tactics in it.

The lead commentator is responsible for the general mood of commentary, which makes him or her a more vital part of a commentary team. I wanted to be the lead after I had established myself as a colour commentator.

Because it's my nature to observe, I was familiar with most of the elements of a live coverage even if they didn't directly affect me. That's why it was not difficult for me to slip into the role of a lead. How good you are in the commentary box can sometimes be gauged by how many lead stints you get.

The one thing that I had to consciously work at was to sound excited. I am not an excitable person – I'm passionate but not excitable. I had to train myself to become excited and animated. I would be passionate and animated when analysing, but to react to a gorgeous cover drive took some conditioning. I am proud that I worked so hard on it that I began to get many lead stints.

The hardest I have had to work in commentary has been in Twenty20 cricket. It's such a high adrenaline activity that a calm quiet voice does not go well with it; and therefore commentary needs to be high octane too. Fortunately, I genuinely love T20 cricket. When some people in production felt I was a bit dull for T20 cricket, I worked on it. I sought out Simon Doull, who gave me a simple piece of advice: While in lead, just focus on reacting to the action, and don't think about too much else. And yes, inflect the voice when there is a spike in action.

I get quite a few lead stints in T20 matches nowadays and I consider that an achievement to be proud of. It's a bit like Cheteshwar Pujara becoming a good T20 player.

The real pinnacle of our job, though, is hosting a live discussion. Having established myself as a lead commentator, this became my next goal. It was Ten Sports that gave me that break. Even when I was not hosting and just commentating, I used to be interested in how it all worked. How the host received instructions from the director through his earpiece. How the host would then manoeuvre the discussion in such a way that the director's next item could be addressed on the show. How sometimes there would be some glitch, and the control room would panic and tell the host not to throw to the next package because it's not ready. The host would still have to wear a smile, a happy face, retract his statement and coolly go back to the discussion while listening to the pandemonium behind the scenes through his earpiece.

The line of conversation also had to head in a certain direction because the videos that will run during the show are pre-decided. They are just waiting for the host to veer the conversation in that direction so that they can be played on the screen. I found all this very challenging. I wanted to give it a shot.

Many kinds of people can become a host, but there is one kind who just can't: the kind who gets easily distracted. Quite a few have tried and failed at this job because they could not handle the commands in the ear while having a conversation with the guest in the studio. It puts them off. I was fortunate on that front. By nature, I don't get easily distracted. In fact, I like the buzz of all activity in the back office loud in my ear so that I know what exactly is going on down there.

Having a chat is the easiest part of the job but keeping it relevant with what the director has planned and incorporating the graphic and video clippings into your discussion without it seeming pre-planned and deliberate is the tough bit.

Once you start hosting and do a reasonable job at it, you earn the respect of your peers. Your colleagues realize you are doing the most difficult job in live broadcasting and you become somewhat like the star of the team. Peter Hutton, who was CEO of Ten Sports, warned me that many a commentator became difficult to handle after he became a host. 'Success' went to their heads.

Steve Norris and John Gaylard, two stalwarts of live cricket production, held my hand as I took my first step in hosting live cricket. I will never forget that first pre-match show we did in

Pakistan in 2004, India's first visit there in fifteen years. It was an elaborate, hyped ninety-minute show, but as it often happens on first days of a tournament, there were last-minute technical snags and we could not rehearse or get a proper sitting with the producer on how we were going to do it. I was still fairly new at hosting, but thankfully, Gaylard's experience came to the fore. 'Sanj, don't worry, I will run you through all this when we are on air,' he said. 'Don't worry, we will be fine.'

And for those ninety minutes it was the controlled, pleasant voice of Gaylard in my ears telling me what was coming next. If there were any accidents down in the production control room (PCR), he did not give me an inkling of it. He just ensured that I was hearing only what I needed to hear as I dived into my preview of a historic Test and series with my two guests Imran Khan and Navjot Singh Sidhu. Viewers would have seen nothing amiss in the show. It was all thanks to Gaylard. After that experience, my confidence got a major boost.

That telecast had an interesting combination of guests. Sidhu, the TV personality, can be quite a bully if he feels he can dominate you. He knew he stood no chance of doing that with Imran. So he made the extreme compromise. Almost all his responses to Imran's statements would begin with, 'As the great man said…' He agreed with everything Imran said, which I found amusing having seen him work before.

Sidhu worked hard on his game, so to speak. On that trip, he did just the studio show, which meant a lot of free time. While the game would be on, he would keep taking notes in this big book. Some of them were legit cricketing observations, rest was what came to be known as Sidhuisms, the wacky one-liners he came up with by improvising on idioms. If he couldn't use one of those Sidhuisms on a particular show, he would find a way to use it on the next. He ensured no Sidhuism went to waste.

Every time he would mention one of his punchlines on air, he would look beamingly at the producer. After a few of those 'Sidhu looks' in his direction, the producer spoke into my earpiece, 'Can you ask Sidhu to stop doing that? He is scaring me.'

But Sidhu was great value, though. It's amazing how he would use all those one-liners on air without fumbling even once. As his colleague, I knew they were not spontaneous, but to the viewer they felt spontaneous. It's not like he looked down to read them.

They might have been an odd combination, but Imran and Sidhu worked well on that show. Once when Pakistan were struggling, Sidhu said, 'Their situation is not as bad as it looks.' Then he paused and said, 'It's worse.'

Imran just collapsed with laughter. It was a while before I could ask Imran a question because he was just unable to speak. It's a side of Imran that not many have seen. Needless to say, Sidhu was thrilled at having made the 'great man' laugh so much.

The other show I remember hosting, and many people do too, was when Imran and Nasser Hussain were my guests. This was also during an India–Pakistan series. We were shooting in Dubai. When Imran arrived at the studio and learnt that Hussain was going to be the guest alongside him, he said, 'What's an Englishman doing in an India Pakistan series?'

By including Hussain, Steve Norris, our head of production, had made a great call. For Steve, television was all about content and he knew Hussain would give great content. And he was right – Hussain turned out to be as passionate about this series as he would be in a series involving England. After a few shows, Imran had had a change of heart.

I still look at those Ten Sports shows with fondness. During that series, Imran kept banging on in the show that Younis Khan should be batting at No. 3, and not lower down in the order. (Younis, however, kept batting down the order.) I remember telling Imran on the show that perhaps he must give up on it and move on. And then when Younis finally moved up the order, he got runs and Pakistan did well.

Imran had that 'I told you so' look and couldn't wait to get on air. As it turned out, it was a short tea-time show, and there were a few commercial packages to get out of the way too. And then a sponsor's interview was forced on us. I just couldn't get to my eager guests in the studio for their views on the session. And one guest was now turning red in anger. It was my worst day in the office. We ran out of time, and I had to throw back to live action without asking my guests a single question in that show.

Imran flung his lapel mic away, and walked out saying, 'What's the point of being here?' He was absolutely right to feel that way. And just to needle me further, the cheeky Hussain said, 'Sanj, it's all your fault.'

Ten Sports had effective and experienced people who'd worked with Channel 9 and Sky Television. So I was in good hands when I started off my second innings. Norris was so intent on having quality content on air that if a conversation was interesting he was happy to let it go on, pushing all the sponsors' packages forward to the next segment. As a result, sometimes in the concluding segment there would be a huge pile-up of pending commercials to run. The analysis, though, would be deeper and revelatory.

I still get compliments for the show we did with Imran and Hussain. In fact, Rahul Dravid told me that this was one show his wife watched diligently, and he too tried to catch it whenever he could. This was incredible to know. I was thrilled that Dravid, who was playing in that series, was one of our viewers.

There have been glitches, though. I remember once when we were ten minutes into a live show and we realized it wasn't our voices but that of the director's that was on air. Gaylard, the director, is well known for his colourful language and that's what now went on air. As a host, I was quite used to his swear words, but imagine putting his usual instructions on air for ten minutes for all viewers in the subcontinent. But guess what – we were lucky that day. In fact, we couldn't believe it – Gaylard didn't swear even once during those ten minutes. He confessed he himself was shocked.

Then there was the Dean Jones–Hashim Amla incident, when Jones was heard by the TV viewers calling Amla a terrorist. There was a bit of history to this. Jones had just returned from a long stint of commentary in the West Indies where the director there had shackled him a bit. He hadn't let Deano be Deano. He kept stopping him from talking excessively. Basically, Jones had been kept on a leash for more than a month, and he was suffering.

After that he was like a prisoner set free when he joined us in Sri Lanka. There was no one here to nag him, and he was now in his element. Interestingly our head of production at Ten Sports had a little chat with us just a couple of days before the incident, asking us to be careful about talking too loudly in between overs, even if it was off the mic, because not everyone is taking commercial breaks and when it's silent you can hear what's being said even when the mics are down. 'Especially you, Deano,' he said, pointing his finger at the man.

To get a few laughs in private, Jones had nicknamed Amla 'a terrorist' on that tour. By all means, this was locker-room humour. As it turned out, Amla took a catch, and a highly excitable Jones thought that we were off air and that everyone was on a commercial break, turned back towards us in the back of the commentary box and said the fateful lines.

Viewers were right to get angry at this, even if the commentator was not saying that into his mic and was under the impression that the whole world had gone for a break. To expect everyone to understand this kind of humour and not receive any backlash for it was also being very naive.

Ten Sports did the right thing. I read out an unconditional apology on behalf of the channel the next day, and Jones was sent home. When he approached Amla to apologize, Amla showed his class by immediately forgiving him for what he had done.

I met Jones that evening. He is quite a character. Anyone in his position would have been completely shattered by the episode; I know I would have been but he seemed to get some kind of kick out of it, not because he was labelled a racist – which he is not – but from the attention he was getting from the incident. At least that's what I thought when I talked to him briefly as he was getting ready to catch the flight back home.

This incident shows the kind of tightrope a commentator walks. A flourishing career could come to an end in the blink of an eye. We want to be funny sometimes, but even while indulging in some humour, we must stay clear of matters of great sensitivity. As commentators we address a universal audience. It's better to stick to a language that offends no one.

There is a video of me on YouTube saying things before we went on air. Which is why I now follow the mantra: once on air, always on air. Even when the mics are down and you think you are in a commercial break. Once you're wired up, in the studio or in the commentary box, there is always someone hearing you or recording you even if the show has not begun. I guess the money we earn doesn't come as easy as some might think.

I miss Wasim Akram when he is not there on the panel. He is a real darling, and great fun to work with in the commentary box. He is like how geniuses are. They can't be expected to suddenly, intricately analyse the performance of others. At least that's what I think. Wasim does not claim to be the best in the business. He does his bit, and he leaves. He is hilarious when it comes to names. He somehow struggles to remember them, and if you have worked long enough with him you know when he needs a bit of help. And when even you are distracted and not around to assist him with names, all he's able to say about someone doing well on the field is, 'That lad is pretty good.'

I have worked with Wasim during a couple of Under-19 tournaments. You can imagine his plight with player names in events like this. He does not take himself too seriously in commentary. Once when he saw me trying to correct something I stated incorrectly on air, he looked at me, confused. 'Why is this so important for you? I have let go of such things many times,' he said with a hearty laugh.

Shoaib Akhtar is also great company in the commentary box. I have worked with him several times for Star Sports' Hindi coverage. He has become a great friend, and I can tell you that he is one of the most talented guys in our world. His reading of the game is quite sharp, and his view of the world, interesting. He too was intrigued by how I went about my work, and would nudge me sometimes.

'Give your mind a rest. How much will you think? How much will you analyse?'

He is right. I take life and work too seriously sometimes. He once insisted we go to his room on the way to dinner to a restaurant on top of our hotel, and I kept saying, 'No, let's meet directly there.' But Shoaib would not budge. I gave in. And then I realized why he wanted me to come – he had got a luxury suite with a 360-degree view of Mumbai city.

Sometimes, out of the blue, I suddenly get a message on WhatsApp from him, 'Hi baby.' Make what you will of it.

*

Commentary is a great job, really. When we are not 'working', we are free to do whatever we please. It could be five days in between two matches and we could be in London, for example, staying in a nice hotel. Basically, it's five days of paid holiday. A lot of commentators spend their free time playing golf. I have stayed away from this occupation because I know it will soon end up being an obsession. It's a bad hobby for a perfectionist. For me those free days are a mix of hitting the gym, watching movies and having great meals at the best restaurants in town.

It is perfect if you can find like-minded company, but it is really important in this profession to like your own company because when you are free, which can be on weekdays, when the rest of the world is working, it's hard to find company all the time. Fortunately, I enjoy my own company. Having room-service meals and watching good television or Netflix is a plan that's hard to beat. Only if something better comes along do I choose otherwise.

My answer to most work opportunities in my free time is a no. I don't like the busy life, rushing from one commitment to the other, like Harsha Bhogle does. He keeps cribbing about how he has no time, but I know, deep down, he likes it. I don't.

For me, this job is custom-made, especially because I don't have to rush from one commitment to another. I played international cricket for nine years, but have commentated on it for much longer. I love my job. I have seen many Indian international-level players try their hand at commentary before moving on to other jobs if it didn't work out for them. Their experience has led me to believe that commentary is a coveted job.

I love commentating for a reason that not many will admit. Yes, it gives me financial security; yes, it lets me stay in touch with the game; but importantly, it gives me visibility. As performers, we become used to this visibility. Anyone who has been a celebrity, big or small, loves to get recognized by people and the perks that come with fame. It's a nice feeling when people you don't know smile at you.

In a way, commentary ensures that people don't forget you. People hardly remember Sidhu the cricketer, for example. Tony Greig is remembered by a generation of fans as merely a commentator – maybe one of the greatest. So commentary gives us that second shot at fame.

I am lucky to have become a commentator and not a coach.

My future as commentator does not depend on the team's performance in matches, which a coach can't control. My future depends on what the viewers think of me. Ever since I have taken up the job, I have been loyal to my viewers because they assess my performance constantly and dictate my future as a commentator.

For me to be good at my job, I make a conscious effort to maintain a certain distance with the players so that I can remain clinical in my assessment of their performances. I have not been close to any current player in my eighteen years as commentator.

Once you know a cricketer too well personally, things can get complicated. He may tend to get hurt when he hears public criticism of him. He would rather expect you to have a private chat with him about it. But players often forget that my loyalty lies with my producer – he must not be denied my views because I prefer sharing it with the player.

I often see fellow commentators walk on to the field on the morning of the match, go out of their way to talk to some player. I wonder then whether they can say the things that ought to be said about that player.

Cricketers too, sometimes, talk about how they are okay with constructive criticism. They lie – I was a cricketer myself. I know.

As players, you are too sensitive about everything, especially criticism, constructive or otherwise, more so when it comes from a cricketer you played with. Cricketers often have this perception that if an ex-cricketer has some critical observations about his game then he must have a personal grudge. Which is why, strained relationships with players is one of our occupational hazards. On the odd occasion when you run in to such a player, you may get a vibe – a cold one. You'd think it's got to do with something you wrote about him, or said on air. I know one player who stopped talking to me ever since I wrote a piece critical of him. What can a commentator do in such cases? You take a deep breath and move on.

That's why it was nice to have Kevin Pietersen join us as a commentator during the World T20 in Sri Lanka in 2012. He came in as someone who had well-documented issues with commentators, but over those two weeks he realized that whatever we said on air was just an observation or analysis for that moment and that we didn't carry any agenda, and more importantly it was not personal. Well, Pietersen's analysis holds true for most of us.

Pietersen left us with words to the effect of: 'Gee, I just realized these guys say things on air and just move on to talking something else. They don't have an elaborate well thought-out plan to destroy a KP or anyone else. We cricketers tend to make a big deal of it, and think that there is a personal vendetta that they have against us.'

Along the way, you meet exceptional people with whom you spend upwards of seven hours a day, with whom you travel over a series, whom you run into at breakfast and gyms. These are my impressions of some of the more exceptional ones that I have worked with.

Tony Greig

My first experience working with Tony Greig was in Sri Lanka for WorldTel. This was my first year in a new profession. I could sense that he was scanning me. He knew me as a player, but now that I was trying to get into his territory he was sussing me out. Did I deserve to be in his world – was I good enough to take some space in the world that he was so passionate about?

Two weeks later I could see that I had passed the Tony Greig test. He told me to my face that I was good, and it started reflecting in the way he worked with me after that. I could have a point of view different from his, and he would be okay with it. The guys he did not approve of would get some heat if they did the same.

He was childlike in many ways, which was also why he made such a name for himself as a TV commentator. His childlike excitement on air was genuine, infectious and distinguished him from the rest. He also had childlike views, mostly about changes in the game, about how to make cricket more exciting. He would share them with excitement whenever he had an audience. If you snubbed his ideas with logic, he would react like a child who had been running around excitedly and had just taken a tumble. He would quickly move on to his next big idea, the next topic of discussion, with the same fervour.

I used to admire him for how upbeat he was about his work every day. Even in a low-key series, say Sri Lanka hosting Bangladesh, when we would assemble in the hotel lobby at 8 a.m. to go to the ground, he never ever looked like a man looking at a long day ahead. He never looked like someone who found it hard to get out of bed or had to drag himself to work. He always dressed the part. I will never forget his walk: the gangly, leaning-forward walk. He never walked slowly; he was always a man on a mission. His mission during commentary assignments was only one. He would often tell me, 'C'mon Sanj, let's lift this coverage today.'

Tony truly believed he could single-handedly raise the quality of the broadcast and generate interest for the cricket he called. That's what made him unique. Every stint that he did was like 'Tony the great' doing everything within his powers to make the coverage great for the viewers. He was a producer's delight. Once you had him in your team, he was there every step of the way to make the coverage better.

All you had to do was give him the most stints in commentary. Childlike that he was, he was pretty sensitive about such things. As long as he was doing more stints than other commentators he was happy. If some other commentator got more time on air, he would get a little grumpy. He believed that his was the voice people wanted to listen to the most.

Tony worked hard; he never came unprepared, even for a minnows' game. He used to carry what looked like a slim pen but was in fact a lead pencil. He would keep taking notes in the little diary that he carried in his pocket.

In his excitement, to take the broadcast to the next level, he would sometimes make embarrassing mistakes but he was never embarrassed by them. He would just say 'correction' and move on.

We were once shooting a studio show in Delhi. It was a chat show that was to be serialized. It was produced by a bright young bunch of TV pros, and Tony was the host. We started rolling. Tony introduced the show, the guests, and began asking a few questions. Seven or eight minutes into the shoot, he suddenly stopped. The producers were talking to him in his earpiece from the control room. And Tony kept nodding and muttering 'yes', 'no, but', 'okay'.

Finally, he said 'okay fine' to the producers, and turned to us and said, 'Look, these chaps think I am talking too much, and that I should take a back seat and let you guys speak more.'

This was a brilliant moment for me in our television business. It's rare for a producer to be able to give feedback to such legends. Most producers are just too intimidated to say anything. Here a thirty-year-old was telling one of the biggest names in cricket commentary to play the role of the interviewer, not the expert, and let the guests speak more.

That thirty-year-old man was Arup Ghosh, now a seasoned TV news professional. Unfortunately, the show was aired on Doordarshan, the government-run broadcaster; it deserved a better platform.

Nevertheless, Tony's response was amazing. He was humble enough to take the feedback and acknowledge that the producer knows what is best for the show. He might have been a domineering presence, but like the producers, he wanted to shoot the best chat show ever. He was a man who stood for great television, and I will always love and respect him for that.

Ian Chappell

I don't think Ian Chappell has uttered even one banal sentence on air. He is not the one to tell you that the first hour of play will be crucial. If he doesn't have anything worthwhile to say, he keeps his mouth shut. Once asked to conduct the toss, all he said was 'all right' and the captain tossed the coin up. He didn't introduce the captains, nor did he say what a great day it was to be alive. When I asked him what he just did, he just said, 'The fans know why I am there, they know who the captains are, so why bother with the other stuff?'

Chappelli – that's what we call him – always speaks his mind. (Although I think his brother, Greg, is far more straightforward than him, which is perhaps why he didn't endear himself to the Indians.) Chappelli, in comparison, is far more pragmatic.

Chappelli once made some critical remarks about Sourav Ganguly on air. Ganguly hit back in his own column the next day. 'Your captain seems very angry with me,' he said to me. 'What next, now?' I asked him. He said, 'Nothing … I will keep looking in his direction; when he is ready to talk, I will talk to him.'

I observed his commentary that day to see if anything had changed, if Ganguly's reaction in the press would tone Chappelli down a little bit. Nothing of the kind happened. His views and approach remained unchanged.

His honesty towards his job is unparalleled.

Chappelli is a true legend of Australian cricket but that does not stop him from doing research on the game like a match reporter would on his first day at work.

Just before the 2016 World T20, I worked with him on some wraparound shows for ESPNcricinfo. He corrected the producers who were briefing him about a change in the West Indies playing eleven.

Most experts just turn up and expect the edit team to worry about such things. Chappelli, however, feels it's his duty as a commentator to know all the stuff related to cricket.

There is one thing common to him and Tony. If they don't respect you as a colleague, it can be difficult working with them. Chappelli, for example, would also take you on, on every view you have but if he likes you and respects you, he lets it pass.

Which is why it's great fun to see how Dean Jones doesn't utter a word in the presence of Chappelli. And believe me, it takes some doing to shut up Dean, who is quite a cricket nerd. He keeps talking incessantly, and when he suddenly goes quiet, we know Chappelli has arrived.

Most of the time, Chappelli shows sound cricket logic, except when it comes to his absolute views on match-fixing. It is fair to say that he comes across as less of an expert but it is a good thing not to be an expert at such things.

Nasser Hussain and Michael Atherton

After the great Channel 9 commentary team led by Richie Benaud, I feel it's Michael Atherton and Nasser Hussain who are the gold standard of cricket commentary. It's because of them and Michael Holding that the Sky commentary team has become the new yardstick.

Most broadcasting companies are adept at producing quality visuals. They can have their own gimmicks. Yet, it is the commentary, the voices that accompany the visuals, that makes the coverage stand out. Nass and Athers are those voices. They have all the qualities needed in top-class, complete commentators.

First, they have the two important Vs to start off with: vocabulary and voice. Only recently have I realized how important voice hygiene is. You could have a lot to share as a commentator, but if your voice is not pleasant you are in trouble. (Kerry Packer once heard a cricketer on his Channel 9 coverage, and had him removed mid-match because he didn't like his voice.)

Second, Nass and Athers both have an analytical mind to boot. They have the overall intelligence to understand the nuances of both the live sport and its commentary. They know the questions that the viewer has about a period of play. They try to think like a viewer, and then use their expertise and their hard work to answer those questions. To viewers, it is almost like someone out there is listening to them and talking to them.

I haven't seen anyone as committed to their day of work as these two are. They don't take things for granted just because they are now reputed, established commentators. This happens to a lot of us. We get lazy. Sometimes we don't watch the game as closely as we're supposed to. We tend to take our eyes off the ball in phases. Not these two. They watch every ball of the day, every day, like a hawk and their mind is ticking all the time.

Nass adds a little more spice to his commentary. He knows that he must entertain even as he informs. He can get abrasive and argumentative while keeping the conversation dignified. I have had my share of debates with him on air, but he is quick to move on from them. I have learnt to do the same.

Sometimes, we Indians get touchy about such things. In our culture, disagreement has come to be equated with disrespect, unfortunately. Once during a one-day game when a fielder hit the stumps, L. Sivaramakrishnan called it a 'good throw'. Nass jumped in: 'C'mon Siva, there was nothing good about that throw. It was unnecessary and that has cost them an extra run.' I could see Siva was taken aback by this whereas Nass had already moved on to the next ball while it took Siva a long time to do the same.

Commentators like them and Mikey compel you to elevate your craft behind the mic. A series with Mikey, Nass and Athers shakes you out of your comfort zone. You have no choice but to be as attentive and perceptive as them. Else, it's difficult having a meaningful stint with them. Commentators should cherish the time they get to spend working with them.

Simon Doull, Pommie Mbangwa and Ian Bishop

Pick these three in your commentary team, and you have the pillars of a live cricket broadcast. They can do everything – host a show, conduct interviews, the toss, post-match presentations, be the lead commentator or the expert, and they are good as commentators for all three formats of the game. If I was a producer, these three would be the most valuable talent on my commentary panel.

Like there is no place for a bad player in a cricket match, I believe there should be no place for a bad commentator in a commentary box even if he has played 500 international matches. Often, we miss out on a lot of exceptional commentary because we insist on them being international cricketers.

One of the best pieces of commentary I heard was during an IPL game that ended in a super over. Doull, Bishop and Shaun

Pollock were on air. That stint was a lesson in commentary, on how to work together as a team, in perfect harmony to give the viewers the best experience possible. Despite being three voices at one time on air, there was no excessive talking. The pictures did most of the job. One person called the action, the second analysed it, and the third tried to pre-empt what was going to happen. It was brilliant.

No one obviously would remember this performance in the commentary box because it is the performance on the field that matters, but if the commentators mess up it can turn the viewers off. Audiences have no time for your playing experience here – here they only care about how you call the game, how you analyse it, and how you keep them engaged. For that, they need not look further than these three.

When Sachin Tendulkar retired from international cricket after his 200th Test match at the Wankhede stadium, it needed a Harsha Bhogle and no one else to sum up the emotions that everyone was feeling at the time. And Harsha did a terrific job.

Harsha has not played Test cricket, but it's for such reasons you need people like him in commentary. I think fans are missing out on possibly great commentators only because production companies these days insist on having former players as commentators.

The day when Sachin retired was the kind of a reminder that even though we all work for money and visibility, it is crucial to have people on board with deep passion for cricket and great television. One of the best producers I have worked with often kept talking about the whole day's coverage in the car ride back home from the game. Yes, you need moneybags around, there would be no broadcast without them, but their number must be kept to the bare minimum. Money-minded people will be at peace working for a builder too, but a creative, sports-minded person will be miserable there. These are the kind of people sports television must retain and embrace.

Some of my best television experience has been with Ten Sports, ESPNStar and ESPNcricinfo. I worked with some smart people here with high educational qualifications who chose to be in cricket media because they loved the sport.

At ESPNcricinfo, we had lawyers, IIM graduates, chartered accountants, talking animatedly about cricket and what we should be discussing on the show. Content that comes from such brainstorming sessions has to be exceptional.

The kind of television we did didn't insult the viewer's intelligence. There are millions of people who are possibly not that educated about cricket, but they are more educated now than they were ten years ago. To presume they need entertainment from outside the sport is insulting their intelligence. If they wanted that, they could switch to another channel. Viewers come to us for sport; we must entertain them with sport.

After all, sport is entertainment of a unique kind. It is human drama, totally unscripted, featuring a high level of skill and real emotions. This combination can't be found anywhere else. With all that at our disposal, we shouldn't have to resort to shortcuts. Stakes in television broadcasting have risen unrealistically; and hence TV channels want to engage the non-cricket fan too. But they should be careful not to put off the real fans in the process – after all, it is they who made cricket a billion-dollar industry in the first place.

I must confess, it bothers me to see a film-star commentating on live international cricket. It's equivalent to a cricketer suddenly appearing on screen while Aamir Khan is in the middle of an intense scene in *Dangal*.

I have seen the role of a commentator change over the years. Back in the day, cricket commentary was also a platform where grievances about the game were freely expressed. But it's tricky to do that now. Cricket commentary is now more about enhancing the viewer's experience, by deploying enriching audio over the visuals. If you're a keen, opinionated observer of the game, it's probably a good idea to express all your passionate views on the game on other platforms, not in the commentary box.

Which is why, I have enjoyed my long association with ESPNcricinfo. To be honest, it's more Sambit Bal, its editor, that I work for than the brand.

I was lucky Sambit came into my life post retirement. He wasn't one who would blindly print everything I wrote – he challenged my first draft, my thoughts, even those about cricket; he urged me to explain and elaborate the opinions made in my columns. Further, he was not ready to carry sweeping statements on the game just because it came from someone who had played the game at the highest level.

I remember once I'd emailed him a piece that I was really proud of. As usual, Sambit came back with certain doubts he wanted clarifications on. I obliged. I thought that was the end of it, but my reply was followed by another email, countering my clarifications.

More emails went back and forth, but he still wasn't satisfied.

I was now angry; this was a piece that I had liked. The next email from me was curt: I said I'd send my article to another publication, if he didn't like it. He immediately called me, and in his typical, soft-spoken and calm manner explained to me why he was asking for clarifications. All he was doing, was making sure there were no lingering doubts in the mind of the reader when he'd read something written by me. 'Your argument has to be fool-proof,' he said. He went on to assure me that emails had gone back and forth several times like that with most of his writers, even his best ones.

Today, after many such columns, Sambit has helped me become a distinct voice compared to the breed of cricketers who think because they have played the game, they can get away by casually saying anything they want.

There is one stint that I did for ESPNcricinfo that I will never forget. In fact, I remember it very fondly. This was in 2013, and ESPNcricinfo was planning to get into videos and not just be a website of the written word.

Sambit had shared this intention with me. It got me very excited. I said, why not do it right now? This was during the India–West Indies series in 2013. There was going to be a lot of attention as it was going to be Tendulkar's 200th Test, also his last.

Sambit got infected by my excitement and agreed immediately. At three days' notice, we decided to dive headlong into pre-match, lunch-time, tea-time and post-match studio shows, the full monty, live on ESPNcricinfo, a website that commanded a minimum viewership of a million.

We were ill prepared for it, but our attitude was that of a go-getter. We had some very bright people on board, so there was a good chance we were going to pull this off.

When you do such shows for a TV channel, the set-up is very elaborate. When we arrive at the ground, it's all arranged and ready for us to go live.

But at ESPNcricinfo, the set-up was very basic, we were using Google Live to get online for God's sake! One of the critical component of live TV shows is the communication between the technical team sitting downstairs in their control room and us, the talent that's in front of the camera. The control room is the nerve centre of any live broadcast.

In the Bangalore office of ESPNcricinfo, our studio, we had a total of three people in our version of the 'control room'.

It dawned on us, unavoidably late, that for the first few days of the Test, we were not going to have the 'earpiece', which relays information from the control room to the talent. It's the lifeline of any live television show.

Raunak Kapoor, one of the most talented young anchors I have seen, was going to be the host. It was his first time, doing something like this live. Like his expert on his television debut in Pakistan, Raunak's foray into live studio shows was also a baptism by fire.

No surprises – the poor fellow was clueless as to what was going to be up next in the show. For hints, he had to sneak a look towards a little board next to the camera while directly looking at it.

That cue board was held up by a senior editorial staff, Nitin Sundar – we called him the clap boy. Depending on the flow of the event, Nitin would hastily write on the board with a marker pen – pitch report, toss, stats, Sachin Tendulkar, batting record, etc.

Had we assigned any lesser talented person than Raunak as anchor, this show wouldn't have been possible. We had only slides to play and no video footage – so the show was all about the spoken word.

There were some false starts. Often we would start the show with great gusto, Raunak opening the episode with some smart lines and I with some pertinent, sharp comments as the expert, only to be told three minutes into the show that we had not gone out live at all. The connection had dropped!

But after a few days, we managed to iron out the glitches; Raunak got his earpiece and we managed to get the 'control room' communication going. Finally, it all began to look like a seasoned cricket show doing live cricket shows for years.

All things set aside, content-wise, it was the best work I have done until now, because Sambit was right next door, like a vigilant officer, and we were all forced to give our best. I remember, for the first few days, Raunak would get summoned to Sambit's office after every show. As for me, I was part-time producer, part-time director, part-time editor of content and graphics, and full-time cricket expert when the show went on air.

The show was called *Match Point*.

BONUS CHAPTER

11

MY DAYS WITH INDIAN CRICKET

MY CRICKET JOURNEY began in the late '70s, at the age of twelve. I soon realized how lucky I was to be growing up and playing cricket in Mumbai. For a young boy with dreams in his eyes of playing for India, the path was well laid in Mumbai – you represented your school and your very first steps into serious cricket were to play in the Giles and the Harris Shield. (By the way, it's only many years later that I realized it was supposed to be pronounced 'jaeels', not 'gaeels'. Remember Ashley Giles?)

During our time, there was tremendous motivation for school cricketers like me to get a hundred or a five-wicket haul, for there would be a headline in the sports pages of the newspaper next day saying 'SANJAY SHINES' or in case of a bowler, something like 'KHANDWALA DEADLY'. At the time, media platforms were few, so these headlines used to get a lot of attention. And boy! What a high that was! Calls from your family and friends would come flooding in, congratulating you on the effort. You felt like a star! Did a twelve-year-old kid need any more inducement to keep playing the game and chasing his dream? No sir! With so many media platforms now, I am not sure a school cricketer's exploits get that much attention, unless, of course, you get a 500 or something, like Prithvi Shaw did.

After school cricket, there was U-15, U-19 then U-22: all important steps to take you closer to your dream. This system, an age-old one, is what really produces quality talent rather than 'academies' that are nowadays mushrooming all over the place. (We used to call them 'nets'. Now they are called 'academies'.)

Again, growing up in Mumbai was a blessing because there were all these marvellous people like Dilip Sardesai and ex-Test stalwarts around ... even on the maidans, at matches, at selection trials to boost your confidence and fuel your ambitions further.

I remember, at one stage, Mr Sardesai being unhappy with my getting out in the 30s and not getting 100s. So, my good friend, Subhash, took it upon himself to remind me of that every time I got out in the 30s and 40s. He would say, 'I am not the believe in the 30s and 40s ... I am the believe in the 100.' They were all these great guys willing you to do better; it was lovely. So, you got the right advice at the right time from the right people, it was all about what you needed to do to succeed at the highest level.

For Mumbaiites, it was always about doing well at the highest level, not the Ranji level. A small-town boy would not have these advantages that we had. At a very impressionable age a wide-eyed young cricketer would get a chance to share a dressing room with current superstars of Indian cricket.

Can you imagine how I must have felt when my idol Sunil Gavaskar was in the same dressing room as me while playing for Dadar Union? I was just fifteen. I watched his every move during the day – my eyes were glued on to him as he went about his business. He must have found me quite creepy, if he had noticed.

Anyway, the next big step was Ranji cricket. And again, the wonderful seniors like Sandeep Patil came to the fore to guide you during an actual cricket match. The tips that you receive from another senior while you are on the field are priceless. (Wasim Akram and Waqar Younis got a heavy dose of this from … well … the current prime minister of Pakistan. It was one important reason for their eventual greatness – their view, not mine.)

Then the twelve-year-old's dream finally came to fruition: I was playing for India. This was the late '80s … the post-Gavaskar era. It remains my regret that this wasn't such a happy chapter in my cricket life. Not so much because of how my own career turned out but because of the climate within the team at the time.

When I entered the Indian team's dressing room, I discovered that there was a divide in the team, like a wall between two groups of players – there were two teams within one.

Thankfully, by the end of my India career these lines blurred. The wall came down eventually and with it also came an improvement of 'Team India's' performance. Team India – I am using the modern terminology, to keep up with the times.

During my time in the Indian team, cricket was still very much an individual sport. If a batsman got a 100 in the first Test of an overseas series, he felt like his job for that series was done. A century or a five-wicket haul in Australia, or England or West Indies was a big thing. It would suffice a player for the entire series. Ambitions at the time were low, and they were even lower for the team – especially abroad. It was all about individual glory. And if the team won in the process, great! Winning was incidental, while every player went about his own business. Indian players were still stars and big brands back home even if the team lost – so there was real motivation to care only about your own performance or be a little selfish.

It was also a time when handling pace and bounce were real issues in Indian cricket. When the opposition had four fast bowlers, it was heart-breaking to see Indian players avoiding such challenges with cunning manoeuvres. For example, when the West Indies came to town, suddenly 'long-term injuries' surfaced amongst players.

This was the '90s – a time and era when there was Pakistan, our neighbouring team led by Imran Khan who set the bar really high. My entire Test career was about me wishing that my Indian team was more like the Pakistan team.

The Pakistan team in those days was a strong one. I remember once when a home series against New Zealand was announced, Imran made his own announcement – that playing the Kiwis at home was a waste of time. 'Pakistan should be touring West Indies and taking on tougher challenges than playing against an ordinary opposition at home,' Imran said. He really thought his team could beat West Indies in the Caribbean and wanted that opportunity.

Here was a team's captain keen to play against West Indies, while in India some players were finding ways to avoid playing them. This was, of course, Pakistan of old. The new Pakistan is a bit like old India – and I am talking here purely about cricket.

To make matters worse, my last years as an India cricketer were spent in the dark cloud of match-fixing. I saw some of my team-mates banned from the game. Once that happened, there was an understandable, nagging suspicion about Indian cricket and the integrity of the Indian team.

This is when Dada – 'Moharaj' as I called him – Sourav Ganguly arrived. And with him in tow was India's first foreign coach, John Wright.

I remember Sourav giving a television interview to Rajdeep Sardesai and even talking about match-fixing in that episode – a brave thing to do considering there was no precedent on this. Most influential players preferred to stay mute on sensitive matters.

Sourav guaranteed a clean Indian team and we trusted him. Post 2000, under Sourav's leadership and a foreign coach, a brighter phase of Indian cricket began. In fact, India played the way I wished they had throughout my playing career. Not only did they compete better overseas, they also had batsmen who were not wary of the short ball anymore – Virender Sehwag, Rahul Dravid, Sachin Tendulkar, V.V.S. Laxman had no issue with pace and bounce and thus we started seeing some fight from India when playing overseas.

India were also turning into a very good ODI team, that too in all conditions. Big sponsorships started coming into Indian cricket and the critical moment for me was the 2003 World Cup when corporate giants like Pepsi invested in the Indian cricket team. India reached the finals of that World Cup in South Africa and it was a very impressive showing considering it was overseas. From there on, the big money stayed parked in Indian cricket.

But India still wasn't winning enough. In the 2003 World Cup final, you could still see signs of insecurities. When India opted to bowl first, it proved to be costly mistake, especially since they had to chase – against an opposition that featured the likes of Glenn McGrath and Brett Lee. So, although under Sourav Ganguly Indian cricket's image became squeaky clean and India played more like a team, it was still not winning enough for a country that had everything going for it.

All that started to change when M.S. Dhoni came in. He got rid of anxiety, a deep-rooted emotion that afflicted India in close matches on the big stage.

Dhoni brought calmness into Indian cricket. Under his leadership, India started winning tight games and most important, started chasing better – the captain himself leading by example.

Dhoni's India team was a formidable ODI side in all conditions, not just at home. The bull run culminated at home when India won the World Cup in 2011. That victory, for me, was India's greatest triumph, in the sense that India were playing in front of a home crowd and with it came the heavy burden of expectations, which they lived up to. Having been a part of the team for the 1996 World Cup – also played at home – I had a personal experience of how tough this is.

Dhoni's incredible calmness brushed off on the others, as he led the way for this great victory. Also, he didn't have a very good bowling attack like we have now. India won the 2011 World Cup despite not being the best bowling side in the world.

If one were to compare India's two World Cup triumphs, I'd say the 1983 win was most significant, while 2011 one was most impressive.

As I mentioned earlier, one thing decisively changed under Dhoni – India started chasing better, no more did it panic in a run chase, like we used to. (I remember the 1992 World Cup game versus Australia at Brisbane as an example.)

Temperamentally too, the Indian team was getting better. Nerves started to disappear. Unlike earlier, this team was now holding its head high even on foreign lands. Their performance may not have skyrocketed with it, but there was more self-belief within the team even when it travelled. Also, we were now looking at a new generation of Indian players who had grown up in a more secure and liberal environment. The changing landscape of the country started reflecting in the attitude and approach of

India's players. They didn't walk into an overseas encounter feeling inferior already.

India was now a better all-round team, it was looking fitter on the field, their fast bowlers were bowling quicker, the batsmen weren't sitting ducks against pace and they ran superbly between wickets.

Running between the wickets: a slightly unacknowledged, undervalued improvement in Indian cricket. Under Dhoni, this aspect of the game got a lot of importance and attention. Like current Indian captain Virat Kohli, Dhoni too believed that running hard between the wickets was the lifeline of any innings. The rare occasions I have seen Dhoni lose his cool have always been when his partner did not respond to his call for an extra run.

India's white-ball cricket was going in the right direction. But somehow, the bane of the '90s, the overseas issues in Tests remained. Indian cricket has not been able to resolve this. A much-weakened Pakistan team still has a better record than India in overseas Tests.

India have just come back from a 4-1 defeat from their England tour. Yes, the scoreline is not indicative of how the actual contest was. But still, it's another overseas loss for India to endure. Interestingly it was the batting that let India down this time. The bowlers kept getting India back in the match and the batsmen kept letting those chances slip. It wasn't temperament that let India's batsmen down in South Africa and England – it was purely a technical problem, specifically defensive technique.

It was simple to see what was going wrong – the batsmen were not leaving enough balls outside the off stump nor were they defending close to the body with a still bat. Now this is the easy part – it's easy to spot such faults but how does one rectify them? That's where things get complicated, because this is now more a cultural thing and it's damn difficult to change cultures, as we know.

Today, Test cricket is played in front of empty stands and the IPL in front of a frenzied crowd of 50,000-plus and has millions watching it on television and online. And guess what? IPL pays better too; in fact, a lot better. Basically, we now have a scenario that's the exact opposite of what it was in the '90s – it's now about playing in the IPL at all costs; player injuries now surface only before and after the IPL. After all, the format offers players fame as well as money. Now, who will say no to this? Also, Test cricket is just too goddamn hard, so it's no wonder many are choosing T20 leagues over Tests.

These days, it appears as if 'playing for the country' is an emotion one feels only when it's an ICC event. There is such random, meaningless country–versus–country cricket going on that playing for the country is not that big a deal anymore nor a matter of great pride like it used to be when matches were fewer. I even cringe a bit when players talk about doing it for the nation … they are just playing a sport.

So, more and more players are training themselves to become good players of the white-ball. When we were growing up, our mind space was occupied only by the long-format game, we trained for it day in and day out, practised leaving balls outside the off stump and the coach behind shrieked in delight saying, 'Well left!' and we felt very proud for having left a ball alone, offering no shot. This aspect of batting is hardly seen nor even needed in white-ball cricket. I wonder how many balls were left alone by batsmen in the eleven editions of the IPL so far?

The quality of Test cricket's main elements or skills – defensive batting, bowling to get a batsman out while he is defending, slip catching – are bound to go down with the unpopularity of Test cricket. After all, why train so hard for something that only a few people watch and that does not pay as much. This is a good analogy for pure classical singing, the Test match version of singing. The world is ever-changing and with it the tastes of people. This is what you call natural forces coming into play and there is nothing anyone can do to stop that.

But try we must. For if not for Test cricket how would we distinguish the men from the boys? It is here I feel that Test cricket is so fortunate that modern cricket's biggest brand, Virat Kohli, loves it immensely and puts his heart and soul into it. To me he looks most driven when he is playing Tests.

Don't get fooled by the crowds you see in England for Test matches; that's an aberration. England loves its heritage, they like holding on to the old. Royalty, for example – they are still so excited by it in the twenty-first century. The English are unique in their tastes and choices.

I travel the cricketing world and see cricket-loving countries struggle to draw crowds for Test matches, but we can – and we must – clutch at straws to keep Test cricket alive. Through social media, for example, we see a lot of young cricket fans following Tests. They understand and value the uniqueness of its unpredictable script, something that other formats can never match. Importantly, Test match performances and results are remembered for a longer time and resonate much more than a half-century in an IPL game which is forgotten in forty-eight hours.

It's not that there is zero interest in Test cricket – just that people can't come to the stadium to watch cricket, or for that matter watch it on TV. That's because we are, well, cocky – we have kept the timings of Tests the same as people's working hours. Gone are the days when people used to bunk office and fill every seat at the Eden Gardens. It's time to be humble and offer Test cricket to fans and viewers as per their convenience. The only way to get more people to watch Test cricket, increase its viewership, its popularity and thereby its quality is through day-night Tests.

And that brings me to the final part of my lecture – taking the bull by its horns. Why are we not playing more day-night Tests when it's a no brainer that the format will attract more viewership?

It's because the players are wary of it – wary of the pink ball, the dew factor at night, etc.

I have always believed conditions are never unfair if it's the same for both sides. Who wouldn't know this better than Mumbai cricketers, who played in the Kanga League, where, along with the ball you sometimes had to handle the muck that came flying with it.

Basically, it means that today we offer perfect conditions for the players to play in, even if it means fewer and fewer spectators are watching.

There was a time when players – at least the India national side players – were at the mercy of the BCCI, the relationship between players and the board was uneasy for a long time. (Remember the clashes over salaries in 1989?) Thank god, all that is in the past. But we must be careful to not go to the other extreme and try and keep players happy, come what may – or at the cost of the game. Take the bull by the horns, I say (nobody seems to do this anymore), do what's best for the game for its long-term health and make the players join in, even if they are reluctant. They will thank us later.

As player, I too had a narrower vision of the game than I have now. While you are at it, taking the bull by the horns, here is another suggestion – for god's sake, do something about the over rates! The amount of milling around that goes on and on, in the cricket field is not funny. No way will this sport find appeal or connect with the youth of today when most of the time they are seeing players walking and standing and having drinks and thus having a devastating effect on over rates. There was a time when nineteen overs were bowled in an hour. Nowadays it's down to twelve! Just a few days back, the Asia Cup final went forty minutes over time! I say, how dare we take people's time for granted like this?

We now have an extra thirty minutes for a fielding side to bowl its quota of ninety overs for the day in Tests because they find it difficult to do it in the stipulated time. And if they are still unable to do it, we say, okay, let it be. It's like a tuition teacher who wants to keep his job tutoring a rich kid. So, essentially, the paying public is sitting an extra thirty minutes and have still not got the 90 overs in the day they came to watch. (Someday, they may ask for a refund for not getting what they were promised.)

The slow over rates, I am afraid, are entirely to do with players being allowed to have their way. Maybe we could have a system like we do in tennis, where they have a timer in between games when players take their little break. In cricket, it can be overs, where the captain is prodded to start the next over and penalized if there is a delay. Whatever works, really – in principle, we must make the game move on faster to stay relevant in today's world when people are eating fast food, seeking faster downloads on the Internet...

Basically, officials need to get a little more officious and yes, strict. Not as strict as the school-cricket umpires that we had, the stone-faced, dictatorial kind – I used to think that the only thing missing was a whip in their hand.

The fact is that there is just too much leniency given to players these days. Hydration, for example, is the new thing. You now have players taking drinks in every little pause in the game – when there is a DRS review, at the fall of a wicket … I have even seen an incoming batsman have a quick drink himself when his partner is having one. Even if a wicket falls in the first over of the day, substitutes rush in with drinks for the fielding team. An official drinks break is taken just after everyone has had a drink few minutes earlier, during a review. My worry, these days, is that a player may get sick because of excessive hydration.

I seriously wonder if players today know the feeling of playing while being thirsty. I know that keeping your water levels up is important, but I also know that a cheetah runs the quickest when it's hungry *and* thirsty.

(This bonus chapter, published in the paperback edition of Imperfect*, is a transcript of the 9th edition of the Dilip Sardesai Lecture, delivered by Sanjay Manjrekar on 1 October 2018 at the C.K. Nayudu Hall, Cricket Club of India, Mumbai.)*

ACKNOWLEDGEMENTS

I DON'T KNOW why, but a lot of people, at various stages of my post retirement life, insisted I should write a book.

Anish Chandy, my literary agent, encouraged me to write my story, was involved in compiling it and brought HarperCollins on board. The team at HarperCollins India – Udayan Mitra, Arcopol Chaudhuri, Bonita Vaz-Shimray have been wonderfully patient collaborators on *Imperfect*. Thanks also to Vickky Idnaani for having to bear with the 'perfectionist'.

There are many people to thank, for the wonderful life I have led.

Yes, I worked pretty hard, and yes, I had some skills too, but if not for the timely and selfless help of these exceptional people, who knows how my life would have turned out.

I think of her first, when I am the happiest, also when I am the saddest – my wife for twenty-six years, Madhavi. Life partner for thirty-two years, she has been with me, hand in hand, through this journey, first as a cricketer and then a commentator.

My children, Devika and Siddharth, are very passionate and creative kids. They have helped me evolve as a person and stay relevant in today's world, so crucial as an opinion maker. We have frequent debates (quarrels, rather) at home and even if she disagrees, Devika is okay with me having the last word. Siddharth never gives up.

Deep down, I am proud that I have raised my children to challenge my thoughts.

My late mother, Rekha and my two sisters, Shubha and Anjali, my brother-in-law, Shashi and my uncle, Ramesh Suvarna have been my strength.

I am also immensely grateful to Mumbai cricket for its love and support. After I lost my father at eighteen, it was Mumbai cricket that became my guardian, as I set out to achieve my dream of becoming a Test cricketer.

Finally, my colleagues in the media, who are my new extended family. I thank them wholeheartedly for their support and for making work so much fun. I could not have done it without them.

INDEX